Editorial

Welcome to the Carp Fishing Encyclopaedia - brought to you in association with Total Carp and Advanced Carp Fishing - the UK's biggest-selling carp fishing magazines.

When we first set out compiling this compendium we thought it couldn't be too difficult. However, it's only when you sit and think about all of the elements involved in carp fishing itself that you realise just how many there are, how huge our sport is and how deeply we carp anglers immerse ourselves in it.

Needless to say, then, that I have spent night after night writing what you see before you and even as I pen this editorial I am thinking of the odd item which has been omitted. That said, I think there is more than enough here to keep you going!

As well as so many of the carpy terms, colloquialisms and even slang, we've listed a selection of high-profile anglers, many of whom appear regularly in our magazines, as well as some of the key products and a sprinkling of the major companies involved in the sport.

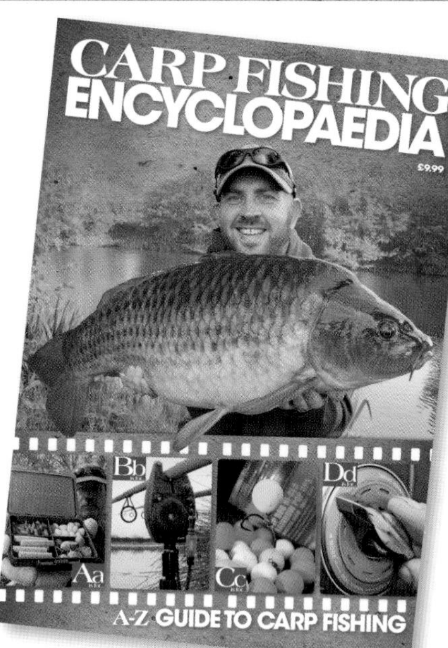

Read it, reference it, take it fishing with you or keep it on your coffee table at home. Whatever the case, I sincerely hope you enjoy the Carp Fishing Encyclopaedia...

Marc Coulson

While every effort has been made to ensure all details are correct, DHP cannot be held responsible for any errors or omissions.

WRITTEN BY:
MARC COULSON
Marc is the editor of the UK's biggest selling carp fishing magazine, Total Carp, and has previously also edited the DHP books Four Seasons Of Carp, volumes 1 and 2, A Carper's Dozen and Let's Go Carp Fishing.

PICS COMPILED BY:
JON BONES &
JASON UMNEY
Jon is the editor of the country's number-one specimen carp fishing magazine, Advanced Carp Fishing, and also co-edited Let's Go Carp Fishing and Four Seasons of Carp, volume 2. Jason is a former editorial assistant with Total Carp magazine.

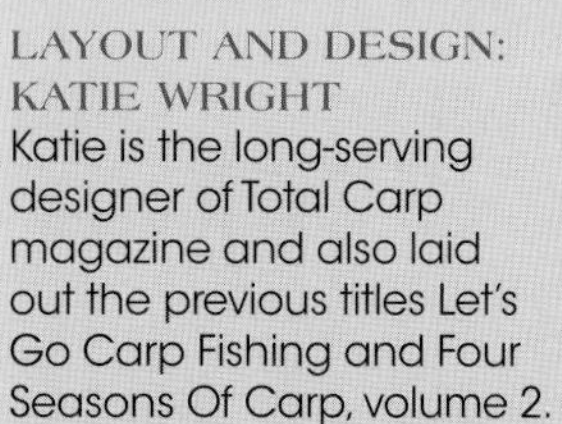

LAYOUT AND DESIGN:
KATIE WRIGHT
Katie is the long-serving designer of Total Carp magazine and also laid out the previous titles Let's Go Carp Fishing and Four Seasons Of Carp, volume 2.

WITH SPECIAL THANKS TO:
Sub editors: David Haynes & Victoria Turnbull
Reprographics: Derek Mooney, Steph Horn and Adam Mason
Advertising sales: Justin Fox & Dean Rothery

Contents

Published by David Hall Publishing Ltd.

Aa
is for...

ACCURACY *(casting)*

It's often been said that 'nearly is not good enough' and this refers to the importance of getting your casting accurate in certain situations. Occasionally, the 'pub chuck' (casting a bait out anywhere in the lake more in hope than expectation) will work but more often than not you will be required to cast accurately if you are catching carp from underwater feature areas. Distance is irrelevant here – accuracy can be everything, be it at 10 yards, 100 yards or more.

ADDITIVES *(bait)*

It would take a separate publication to list all of the additives that go into the myriad of modern carp baits, but they are generally grouped into fishmeals, birdfoods, milk proteins, flavours, oils and other ingredients.

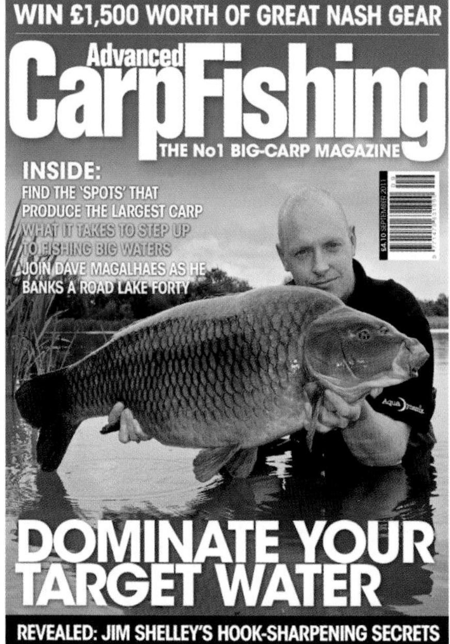
WIN £1,500 WORTH OF GREAT NASH GEAR
Advanced
CarpFishing
THE No1 BIG-CARP MAGAZINE
INSIDE:
FIND THE 'SPOTS' THAT PRODUCE THE LARGEST CARP
WHAT IT TAKES TO STEP UP TO FISHING BIG WATERS
JOIN DAVE MAGALHAES AS HE BANKS A ROAD LAKE FORTY
DOMINATE YOUR TARGET WATER
REVEALED: JIM SHELLEY'S HOOK-SHARPENING SECRETS

ADVANCED CARP FISHING *(magazine)*

The biggest-selling specimen carp fishing magazine, this is the read for the out-and-out big-carp angler. ACF is packed with features from the biggest names, about big carp, big-carp venues and the tactics employed by those who target these lakes and the specimens within.

On sale around the middle of each month and published by David Hall Publishing, ACF has a circulation (at time of publication) of around 16,000.

AIR-DRIED BAITS

This refers to boilies that have been left out in the air in order to remove the moisture. This is done for two main reasons, namely to help preserve these baits and to make them harder. Preservation is usually to make them last longer, and stay fresher, on longer sessions both at home and on trips abroad. Making a bait harder (this can also be achieved with certain additives or by ultra-long-term soaking in a bait dip) helps keep the bait intact when fishing waters that have lots of small fish, crays or other creatures which can whittle a softer bait down.

AIR-DRYING BAG

These are mesh bags which are used to air dry baits and can be hung in your garage prior to a trip (or in the airing cupboard if your missus allows!). They can also be hung from a tree or suchlike when in a fishing situation.

ANGLING

Another word for fishing, usually only relating to non-game fishing activities. Includes carp angling.

ANGLING LINES *(company)*

Provider of carp and catfish fishing holidays in France and beyond. Website: *www.anglinglines.com*

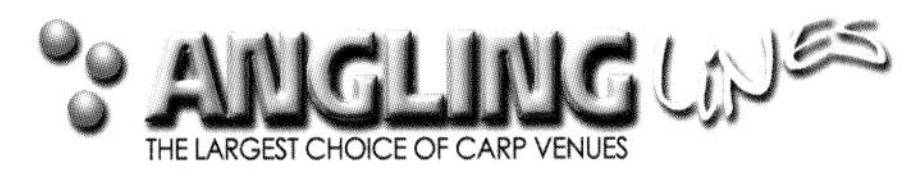

ANISEED

A hugely successful bait additive, which has been used for many years in boilie recipes and especially in particle mixes.

ANTI-EJECT RIGS

Many anglers believe that carp attempt to blow out, or 'eject' a baited rig in the process of picking the hook bait up off the lake bed. Anti-eject rigs feature all manner of components and mechanics to attempt to avoid this ejection of the bait by the carp. Sliding rig rings, weighted putty, long hairs, tubing and many other items are employed in a bid to create the perfect anti-eject rig. Until now, no rig is said to be absolutely flawless in this respect, otherwise we would all be using it!

ANTI-TANGLE

It is important that, when cast out, your rig does not tangle, that is become a knotted mess of line which will not be effective in achieving a bite. So, all of the modern carp companies have developed a huge variety of items to help avoid tangles, from rig materials right through to leaders and tubing.

ANTISEPTIC

Used to treat hook marks and any other blemishes on a carp, either in the mouth or on the flanks. These blemishes are not necessarily caused by anglers; carp often create their own wounds when spawning and rubbing themselves, so we carp anglers try and help where possible. You should never go fishing without a carp-care kit, which will usually include an antiseptic lotion of some description.

AQUA PRODUCTS *(company)*

Manufacturer of bivvies, luggage, sleeping bags and clothing, as well as associated accessories.
Website: *www.aquaproducts.co.uk*

APPS *(Apple)*

Software programmes for iPhones, iPads and suchlike, a variety of which are aimed at the modern carp angler. Check out the Total Carp and Advanced Carp Fishing apps on the Apple App Store now.

AQUACULTURE
The study of underwater life and, in our case, fish and their environment. Sparsholt is perhaps the best-known college offering all manner of courses in aquaculture and related subjects.

ARTIFICIAL BAITS
All the rage in recent years, these are made from various materials, including plastics, rubbers and starch-based substances, and are designed to replicate boilies, sweetcorn, maggots, pellets and even water snails. There is some debate as to the safety of these baits, as they are seen as an eternal temptation when attached to a rig, which may have become parted from an angler's other tackle.

Many argue that it's not just the visual imitation of the bait that attracts the carp's attention. The colour of the baits can play a part and many anglers use a piece of bright artificial corn or suchlike to 'tip' a boilie hook bait in order to make it stand out among free offerings. Some even argue that the ethers in the rubbers themselves are a carp attractor.

ATTRACTANTS
Bait additives, which heighten the fish's senses and induce a feeding response or similar. There are literally hundreds of different ones available in modern bait ingredients and additives.

AVID CARP *(company)*
Manufacturer of bivvies, luggage, chairs and bedchairs, terminal tackle and associated products.
Website: *www.avidcarp.co.uk*

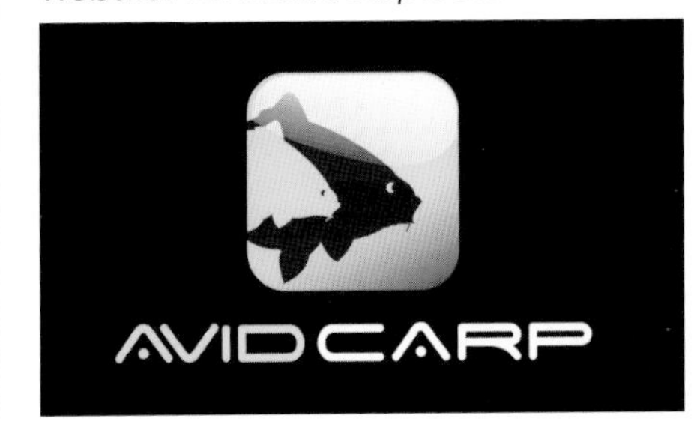

Bb is for...

BACK LEADS
Small leads which are attached to the main line and which keep this line pinned to the lake bed. This is done for two main reasons, namely to disguise the presence of the line to passing fish, and to avoid fish picking up an angler's second or third line while being played to the bank. There are many different styles of back lead available to the modern carp angler.

Essentially these fall into two categories, free and captive. The free back leads attach to the line and can then be slid down to any point between you and your leader, by manipulating the line angle. Captive back leads are attached to a short cord and only slide down into the margins. These can often detach when necessary and the cord is used to then retrieve them after use.

BACK RESTS
(aka butt rests, butt grips)
A U-shaped item which sits on the rear buzz bar or bankstick and which the butt of the rod rests in while fishing. These can be simple items that the rod rests on and no more, or they can often be a little more involved and offer stronger gripping of the butt when fishing snags and the like, or for more general, secure use.

BAIT
An umbrella term for the masses of edible and artificial items that are used to attract fish to your rig. Many of the more popular baits are covered individually in this encyclopaedia.

BAIT BANDS
Rubber bands which can be used to attach various baits to the hook or similar. Often used when floater fishing with dog biscuits, they are also suited to other baits which can be difficult to pierce, such as pellets.

BAIT BOATS

Radio-controlled boats, which are used to despatch free bait and baited rigs. They feature single or twin hoppers (these are the compartments which hold the bait itself) and are usually powered either by propellers or water-jet systems.

There are many companies that manufacture bait boats these days and the models themselves vary in size, features and price.

Many anglers frown upon the use of bait boats and say that they reduce the skill of an angler using one, as no casting is required to get the bait into the correct areas. However, in the right situation and when used safely, they can help carp anglers enjoy success.

BAIT SPOON

As the name suggests this is a spoon-shaped article which attaches to the end of a pole and is used to ladle bait into spots which are otherwise inaccessible to the carp angler. Although a short-range tactic, they can be extremely useful when fishing under overhanging trees and other marginal cover. Modern versions can be attached to carbon poles up to 16 metres in length.

BAKER, BOB

Founder of pioneering bait company Richworth, one of the earliest manufacturers of boilies including the original Tutti Frutti, which took waters apart back in the late 1970s and early 1980s and remains a popular and successful bait today.

BANKSTICKS

Support for rods, either in single fashion with the individual bite alarms and rests attached or as the support for buzz bars. Come in all lengths and made from carbon, stainless steel, aluminium and suchlike.

BANS

This refers to equipment, baits and tactics that are not allowed to be utilised at certain fisheries. The most common of these fishery bans include particles, nuts, leadcore, barbed or barbless hooks, braided main lines and even boilies.

Sadly, on many waters these bans (and other fishery rules) are knee-jerk reactions to isolated cases of neglect or misuse, sometimes even at other fisheries. Generally, if all baits, tackle and tactics are used correctly and safely, there should be no problem with them.

BARB *(hook)*

The barb is the often-tiny backward-facing protrusion on the inside of the hook's bend. Modern hooks tend to feature micro barbs, as opposed to some of the much bigger barbs found on older carp hooks.

BARBED /BARBLESS *(hooks)*

The term used to describe a hook depending on whether or not it features a barb. Many waters only allow barbless hooks, although an increasing number are going the other way these days and insisting on barbed hooks only. There is a debate as to which version is safer for the carp and, as these varying rules suggest, the argument continues.

BERKLEY *(company)*

Manufacturer and supplier of fishing lines, including braid, monofilament and fluorocarbon, as well as many other accessories and, more recently, the Gulp! Range of carp baits. Website: *www.berkley-fishing.co.uk*

BEDCHAIR

Fold-out bed which can double as a chair, but normally is only used to sleep on. The early versions back in 1982 were the brainchild of Cliff Fox of Fox International and, today, very many manufacturers produce them in some shape or form. Technology has seen advancements in frame build and design as well as many different mattress variations. They even come in different sizes. A far cry from the originals all those years ago.

BIRDS

Yes, birds. We all know what they are, but in context the water-borne ones can be a royal pain for the carp angler and often steal baits, disturb lines and cause a general niusance.

BITES *(from fish)*

The act of a fish picking up and swimming off with your baited rig. Signalled by movement in the line or bobbin, and by sound from a bite alarm.

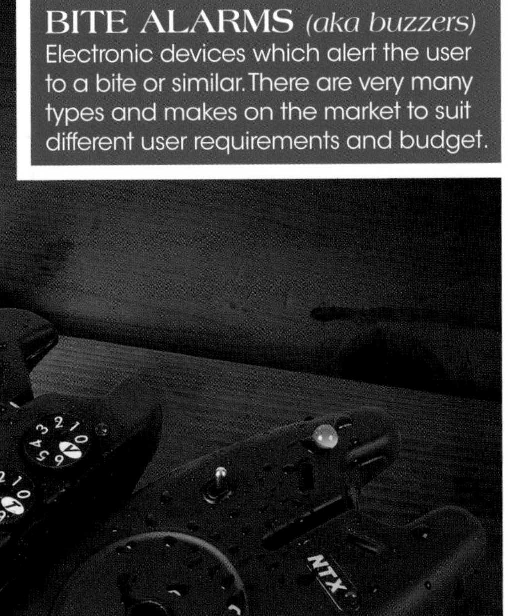

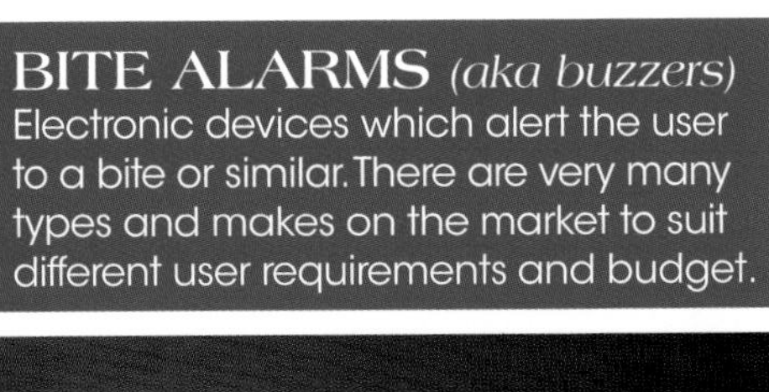

BITE ALARMS *(aka buzzers)*

Electronic devices which alert the user to a bite or similar. There are very many types and makes on the market to suit different user requirements and budget.

BIVVY

From the term bivouac, a bivvy is a tent-like shelter for carp anglers, usually green in colour to blend in with anglers' surroundings. There are versions designed for single or multiple occupancy and there are literally hundreds of different models on the market. These have evolved over many years and, today, the most popular design is known as a pram-hood.

Lots of associated products are designed for use in and around the bivvy such as bivvy lights, bivvy tables and bivvy mats.

BLOOD KNOT

A knot which can be used to attach hooks or swivels to line. Best suited to monofilament lines it also works with braids. There are full and half versions of this extremely popular knot.

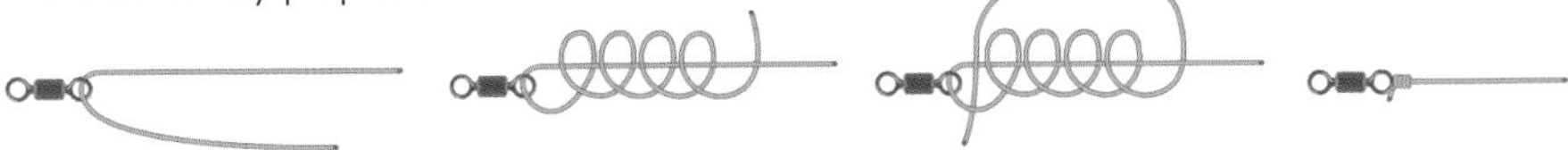

BLOODWORM

The larvae of the midge or gnat, bloodworm forms an element of the carp's natural diet. Although bloodworm in its raw form is rarely used by carp anglers, bloodworm in various forms is used as a successful ingredient and additive in many carp baits.

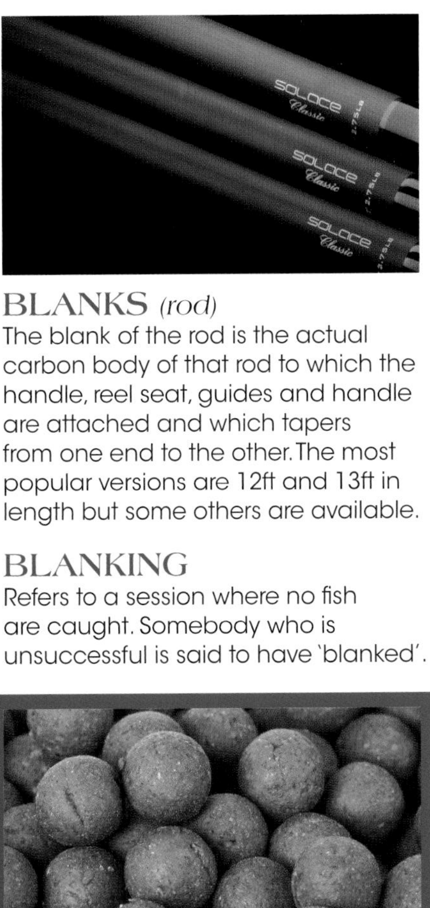

BLANKS *(rod)*

The blank of the rod is the actual carbon body of that rod to which the handle, reel seat, guides and handle are attached and which tapers from one end to the other. The most popular versions are 12ft and 13ft in length but some others are available.

BLANKING

Refers to a session where no fish are caught. Somebody who is unsuccessful is said to have 'blanked'.

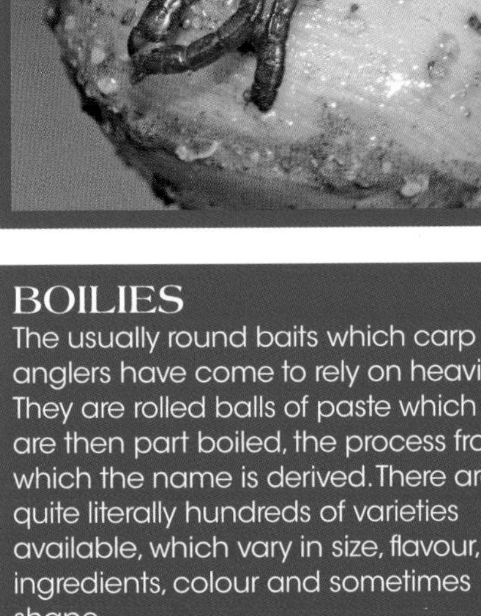

BOILIES

The usually round baits which carp anglers have come to rely on heavily. They are rolled balls of paste which are then part boiled, the process from which the name is derived. There are quite literally hundreds of varieties available, which vary in size, flavour, ingredients, colour and sometimes shape.

BONES, JONATHAN
Editor of Advanced Carp Fishing magazine and co-compiler of this encyclopaedia.

BRAID
Fishing line utilised as both a main line and hook-link material and which is produced by the intertwining of two or more composite lines. Braided lines boast near-zero stretch and usually feature a diameter much thinner than monofilament for a similar breaking strain. There are floating, neutral buoyancy and sinking braids and some differ in profile.

BUCKETS
What many carp anglers use to store bait in while fishing and in between trips. Airtight lids offer obvious advantages compared, say, to an open bag. Rigid buckets also double up as handy seats while fishing.

The more image-conscious carp angler will opt for green or even camou-patterned buckets, with the opposite end of the scale being 'white-bucket man'!

BUTT RING
The first, and usually largest, guide on a fishing rod. This guide is nearest the reel and is designed to begin the process of reducing the coil of line from the reel and aligning it with the rest of the guides and blank. Most popularly 40mm or 50mm in diameter.

BUZZER BARS
Bars which bite alarms (or buzzers) and back rests are attached to and which are then attached to bank sticks for rod support. Generally these house two, three or four rods at a time and are often made from stainless steel, aluminium or even carbon.

CAMERA

You'll need one for taking photographs of that fish of a lifetime. Most carp anglers will carry a compact digital camera which takes up little room in their rucksack or holdall. Some anglers will buy a camera with self-take capabilities, ideal for when fishing alone or when nobody is around to take the photos. A tripod is also necessary to accompany a self-take camera, but sometimes a bucket or similar will suffice to support the camera itself.

If we could give one tip when choosing a camera it would be to find something that is easy to use. Remember, no matter how capable a photographer you might be, if you are asking a complete novice to take photos for you then the camera shouldn't require a degree in rocket science to use it!

CAMOUFLAGE
(aka camou)

Although probably less prevalent in more recent years, camou clothing has long been the rage with the modern carp angler. In fact, even back in the earlier days of carp fishing, army-style fatigues were common, but in the last decade there have been numerous camouflage patterns crossing over from the hunting fraternity into carp fishing. Whether or not you need to be hidden from all and sundry is the choice of the individual, but many will say that it cannot do any harm, so why not!

CANADIAN PONDWEED

Growing to almost three metres in length, *Elodea canadensis* is a prolific weed in many UK venues, especially those that boast clear waters. Originally introduced to the UK, from North America, in the early 19th century, it has thrived here ever since and is one of the most commonly occurring aquatic weeds which carp anglers face.

Carp like to inhabit areas of Canadian pondweed and can find many of their natural food items in and around it, such as water snails.

CANALS

The UK's canals are increasingly populated by carp and are often worth a try for a bite or two. A bonus of fishing the canals is that many stretches can be fished for free, however you should try and check this before angling.

CARP

Once you've caught one there is no going back. Only the barbel can match the fighting power of *Cyprinus carpio* in terms of the UK's native freshwater species and it is this, combined with their propensity to grow to huge proportions, which makes the carp the favoured quarry of so many modern anglers. There are three main categories of the king carp (the species for which we fish), namely common, mirror and leather, each of which is covered elsewhere in this book.

CATCH PICS
Cherished photographs of our favourite captures. Carp anglers place large value on their photographs, given that we always slip the carp back into their watery home after capture. We might never again be acquainted with any particular carp that we catch, so a good photograph is essential to chronicle the magical occasion.

CASTING
The motion of using the fishing rod to send the baited rig out into the lake. Casts can be underarm at very short range, or more likely will be made from behind the angler in a motion that sends the rod above the head and forwards towards the target destination.

CATAPULT
Often referred to, outside of angling, as a slingshot, it's used to deposit bait out into the lake at ranges normally up to 50 to 60 yards or so. With the right catapult, some anglers can send certain baits much further than this, but most longer-range baiting will be done using a spod or throwing stick, which you will find elsewhere in this book.

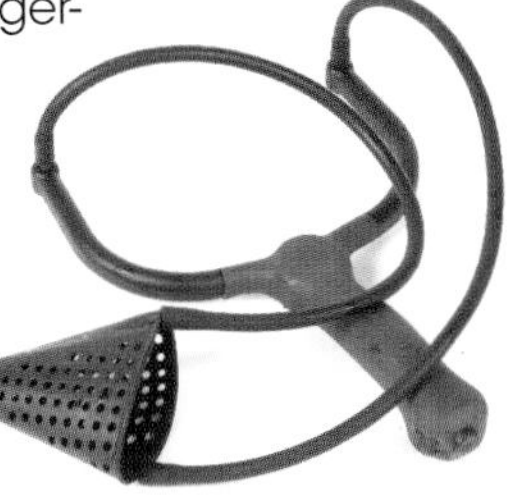

CC MOORE *(company)*
Dorset-based bait company, responsible for such boilies as Odyssey XXX, N-Gage XP and Meteor. CC Moore also produces a huge range of pellets, particles and other carp fishing baits. Website: *www.ccmoore.com*

CELEBRITY *(carp angler)*
Very many of the country's famous citizens enjoy a spot of carp fishing, and some of them are positively mad for it. We on Total Carp magazine have featured film stars, including Tom Felton of Draco Malfoy fame; footballers, including John Terry, Lee Bowyer and Bobby Zamora and other well-known dignitaries including Chris Tarrant and even N-Dubz front man Dappy, enjoying their carp fishing.

CHOD
Colloquial term for the detritus and debris laying on the lake bed. Specific rigs and terminal tackle have been developed to overcome the problems of presenting a hook bait over 'chod' and many of these have become staple elements of many carp anglers' armoury.

CHAPEL BAITS *(company)*
Bait manufacturer whose products include Greedy Pig carp baits. Website: *www.chapelbaits.co.uk*

CHOD RIG
All the rage with many modern carp anglers, the chod rig has been developed to cope with the problems that fishing over 'chod' can create. The bait sits up proud of the lake bed and, so, can be easily found by the carp. Many anglers use chod rigs almost exclusively for their carp fishing, such is its effectiveness. However, it has been designed for this specific purpose, and other rigs are better in other cases.

CHILLCOTT, IAN
Well-known and much-loved carp angler and co-founder of the English Carp Heritage Organisation (ECHO). 'Chilly' is also a prolific writer, with two books already to his name, and has regular series' in both Total Carp and Advanced Carp Fishing magazines.

CHOPPED BAITS
(aka Chops)

This is the term used to describe broken boilies which are an effective carp bait. They make an especially good addition to spod mixes and can also be used inside a PVA bag.

CHUB *(company)*

Manufacturer of carp rods, luggage, clothing, bedchairs, sleeping bags and much more. Chub also forms part of the Chub & Greys Carp Academy. Website: *www.chubfishing.com*

CLOSE SEASON

March 15th - June 15th

Traditionally, the nation's waters were closed to angling between March 15th and June 15th. However, in modern times this ban was lifted from canals and stillwaters and, at the time of writing, only applied to rivers.

The debate rages about the relevance of the river close season, as it only applies to anglers and not other waterway users such as canoeists and ramblers.

Many individual venues will impose their own close seasons, for varying reasons including allowing the resident fish to spawn undisturbed by anglers, but also winter closures can be common.

COLOURED WATER

This is the term used to describe water that is cloudy in appearance and not clear. This cloudiness is caused by many things, including disturbed lake-bed materials, and are more associated with well-stocked venues with lots of active carp in.

Isolated areas of coloured water in otherwise clear lakes can be a sign of feeding carp and so should be investigated by the carp angler.

The nature of the ground on which lakes are dug will also have a huge effect on water clarity, as can recent weather conditions.

COMMON *(carp)*

At one time this type of carp, covered almost entirely with uniform scales, was indeed the most common carp in UK waters. Originally introduced by monks, and used as a food source, they were selectively bred to produce slightly different 'strains' with fewer scales, known as mirror carp. These 'mirrors' have now become the predominant variety of carp in this country.

CONFIDENCE

The single most important element in the carp angler's armoury. A confident angler is often a more efficient angler and this confidence is borne from experience, practice and, very often, trial and error.

COOL BAGS

Carp anglers often use the freshest bait possible and their baits are kept this way for longer by being stored in a cool bag. There are also dedicated cool bags for storing food in good condition for longer spells on the bank. A lot of these cool bags even have crockery and cutlery included and are more like picnic bags than fishing holdalls.

In many of our tests we have found that even the better versions only work efficiently with the addition of freezer blocks, so bear that in mind if you are in the market for one.

CORK

Used in very many forms by the modern carp angler. Small, barrel-shaped plugs can be used to balance hook baits and even to mimic floating-pellet hook baits when surface fishing. Cork balls can be wrapped with boilie paste before boiling to create balanced baits or what are referred to as 'cork-ball pop-ups'. Finally, cork dust can be added to boilie mixes to once again achieve a balanced or buoyant bait. A highly versatile, simple item in the carp angler's armoury.

COTSWOLD BAIT CREATIONS *(company)*

Bait manufacturer, whose products include a range of prepared, PVA-friendly particles; liquids and boilies. Website: *www.cotswoldbaits.com*

COULSON, MARC

Editor of Total Carp magazine, the UK's biggest-selling carp fishing monthly carp fishing magazine. Marc is also the author of this encyclopaedia.

CRIMPS

A product that has been adopted from the electronics industry, crimps can be used to form loops in stiff lines which otherwise may be difficult to tie with loop knots and such like. They are also used extensively by predator anglers to join wire traces and suchlike.

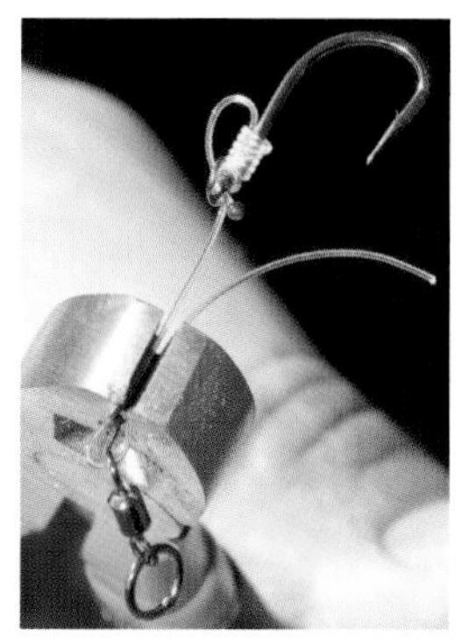

CRITICALLY BALANCED *(baits)*

These are hook baits which have been created or manipulated to be almost neutrally buoyant or, at least, sink extremely slowly. Many anglers believe that these baits, by negating the weight of the hook, behave more like the free offerings and, so, are more readily accepted by feeding carp.

CRAYFISH

Similar to small lobsters in appearance, crayfish inhabit an increasing number of the UK's rivers and stillwaters and can play havoc with carp anglers' rigs and baits. The indigenous species of British crays have been pushed out by the more aggressive signal crayfish, identifiable by their often bright-red claws. This American species has begun to replace the UK's crays in a similar way to which grey squirrels have dominated and then replaced the red squirrel in the UK.

Crayfish will often tangle rigs and damage and even steal hook baits and many tactics have been employed by carp anglers to overcome them. These include using stiffer hook links, which do not tangle so easily; shrouding hook baits in mesh material similar to ladies' tights and the use of alternative baits such as plastic imitations and hard tiger nuts. Whatever the case, fishing a venue inhabited by crayfish can be an arduous exercise. The flip side is that crayfish, when they shed their skins each year, provide a protein-rich food course for the larger coarse fish, including carp. The huge increases in barbel and chub weights in the UK's rivers has been largely attributed to the boom in crayfish populations in many areas.

CYPRINID

Another term for a member of the carp family, although not necessarily the king carp, which this book largely covers. Other cyprinids include crucian carp and even goldfish!

The early morning mist rises over an idyllic English carp pool...

A B C D E F G H I J K L M N O P Q R S T U V W X Y Z

DAIWA *(company)*
Manufacturer of market-leading fishing reels, as well as rods, luggage and other angling equipment.
Website: *www.daiwasports.co.uk*

DANGLERS
Along with bobbins, this is a colloquial term for bite indicators such as hangers.

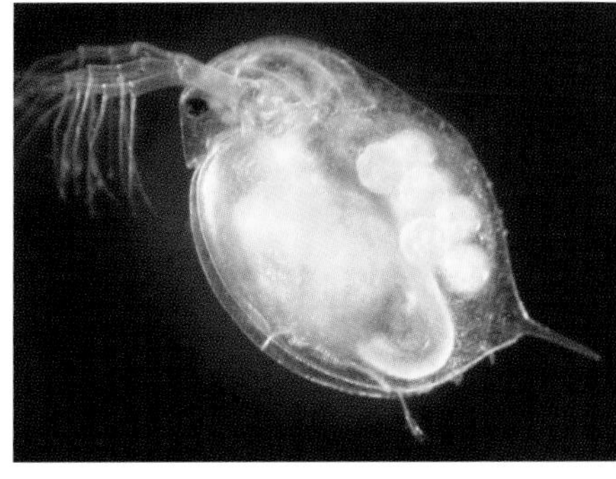

DAPHNIA
Microscopic, plankton-like crustaceans, which occur naturally in freshwater and often in huge numbers, forming daphnia clouds. These are fed on readily by carp and dried versions are even used in some carp-bait recipes.

DAY TICKET
Issued as proof of payment at open-access fishing venues. Such venues are known as 'day-ticket lakes' and are often featured in magazine articles. These are by far the most popular venues and can demand certain 'day-ticket tactics' and suchlike. Day ticket itself has become a term applied to all manner of bait items, initially to appeal to the type of angler who fishes day-ticket waters.

DETRITUS
Although strictly relating to dead or spent organic matter, detritus has also become a commonly used term for general loose matter on lake beds.

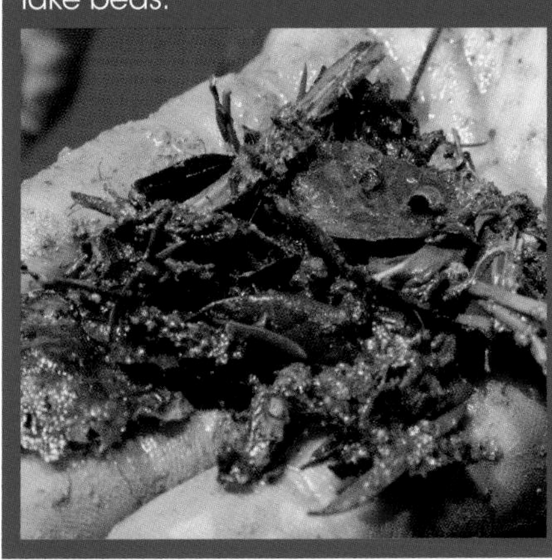

DELKIM *(company)*
British manufacturer of market-leading bite alarms and associated products. Website: *www.delkim.co.uk*

DIEM *(company)*
Maker of ultra-cool clothing, designed for carp anglers on and off the bank. Website: *www.diem-angling.com*

DINTON PASTURES
Well-known carp water controlled by Wokingham Council and situated near Reading, UK. There are two waters on the site, Black Swan and White Swan, the latter being the well-known one which is popular with big-carp chasing anglers. Black Swan offers a bit more of the unknown.

DIPS
Liquids, which are often packed with carp attractors and which are used to give an extra layer of attraction to boilies and suchlike. Generally, hook baits are 'dipped' prior to casting out. When baits are left in these liquids for a longer period they generally become known as 'soaks'.

DINGHY
Inflatable boat used by some carp anglers when mapping out lake beds, baiting up or lowering rigs on to the bottom when fishing. Remember, never go out in a boat unless you're wearing a life jacket and always make somebody else aware of your intention to do so.

DISSOLVING FOAM
Often mistakenly referred to as PVA Foam, this is actually made from a starch-based product and is predominantly used as packing in parcels. The modern carp angler uses it by attaching a nugget to the hook prior to casting out. This protects the hook point on the cast and as it descends through the water. The buoyant foam also keeps the hook bait proud of the bottom, reducing the chances of tangles, before it dissolves and disappears.

DISTANCE FISHING
(aka long-range fishing)
The practice of casting your baited rig out at long distances and fishing further out than those other anglers who are either incapable or not minded to fish at such ranges. Some carp anglers, such as Terry Edmonds and Mark Hutchinson, hold distance-casting records and can launch leads well beyond the 200m mark.

Long-range fishing is often an effective tactic on larger lakes where angler pressure closer to the bank can see fish move out into the relatively safer water further out. In these instances, those anglers who can cast to these fish can often enjoy unrivalled success.

DONKEY CHOKERS

A term used colloquially to describe oversized carp baits, usually anything larger than 24mm in diameter.

D-RIG

This is formed when using stiff hook-link materials as an alternative to the hair rig. The tag end of a knotless knot (on which a hair loop might otherwise be tied) is passed back through the back of the hook's eye and then 'blobbed' with a lighter to prevent it slipping back again. A rig ring is incoporated, to which the hook bait is tied.

Snapshot of a D-rig

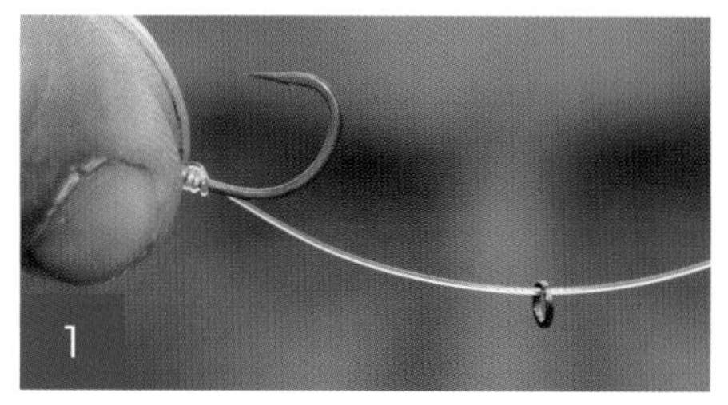

Tie a hair rig with a tag end and thread on a rig ring.

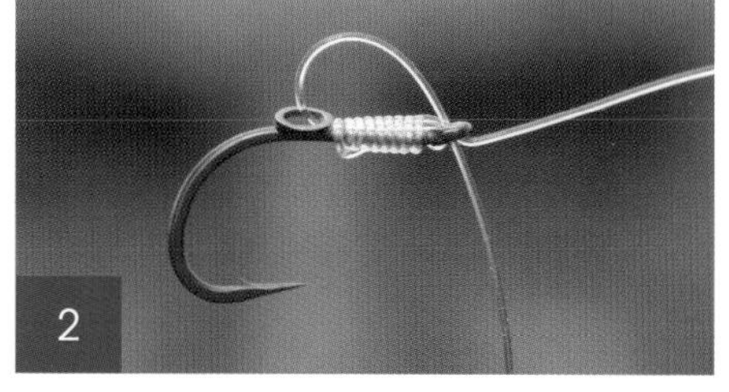

Pass the tag through the back of the hook's eye, like so.

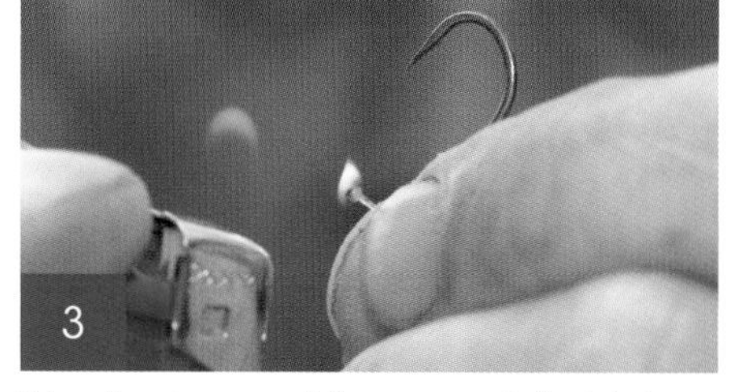

Trim the tag and then carefully blob the end with a lighter.

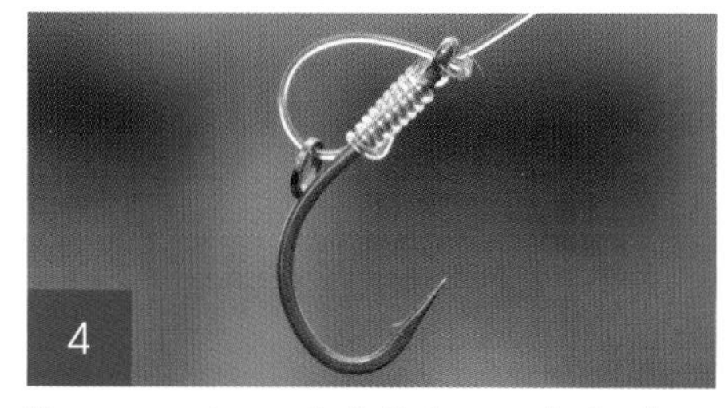

There you have it. A D-rig ready for the hook bait to be tied on to the ring.

DOVE, TOM

Prolific young carp angler from Essex and a regular in many of the various angling publications.

DROP BACK

This refers to the indication of a bite at the bobbins, where the indicator falls towards the ground rather than be pulled up tight to the bite alarm. It is caused by a fish which has picked up the baited rig moving towards the angler rather than away and the resulting slack in the line means the bobbin falls rather than rises.

DRAG

This is the control mechanism over the rate at which line can be pulled off a reel's spool, under tension. Also known as the clutch.

DUCKS

Waterfowl, which carp anglers inevitably come into contact with on a regular basis. Some ducks can be detrimental to the efforts of the carp angler, particularly those such as tufted ducks, which can dive to significant depths to pick up anglers' baits.

DUMBBELLS

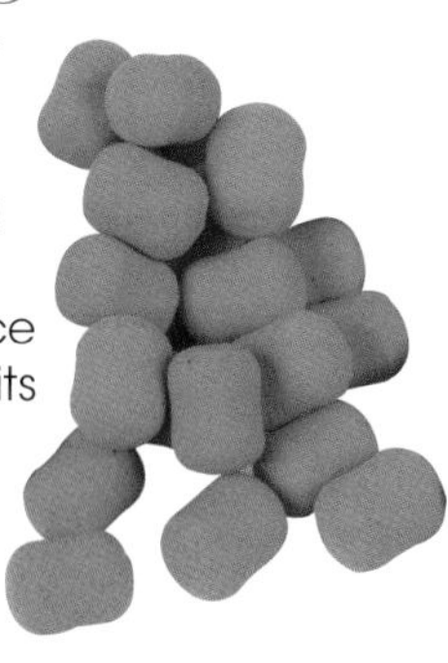

This refers to barrel-shaped boilies, as opposed to the usual spherical baits. Many bait companies produce dumbbell hook baits and a growing number also produce these for use as freebies.

DUSTBIN, THE

Well-known and much-written-about near-leather carp that resided in Yateley Car Park Lake and which reached a top weight of 44lb 8oz. Famous captors include Ian Chillcott, Gaz Fareham and James Davies, pictured below, who caught the magnificent fish twice!

DVDS

Increasingly popular media, bringing magazine-style content in moving form to the masses.

DYNAMITE BAITS

Midlands-based bait manufacturer, responsible for such baits as The Source, Savoury Spice, Chocolate Malt & Tiger Nut and Spicy Peanut. Website: *www.dynamitebaits.com*

ECHO *(The English Carp Heritage Organisation)*

Originally formed by carp anglers Keith Jenkins and Ian Chillcott, ECHO set out to highlight the plight of illegally imported carp. Many felt that the group was little more than a 'band of brothers' at first, but it soon evolved and became more vociferous and effective in its mandate.

ECHO now sits as an important member of the Angling Trust and is run by a group of devoted volunteers, including long-standing member Ruth Lockwood, who now chairs the committee.

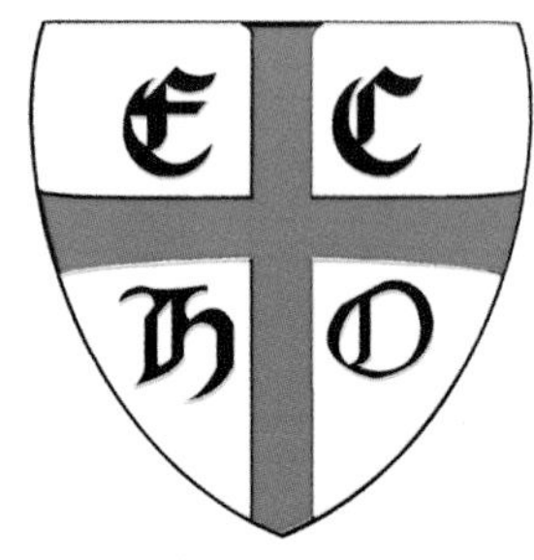

EFFORT

You will get more out of carp fishing, the more you put into carp fishing. Effort equals reward and very often the most impressive and successful carp anglers are those who combine immense effort with their ability, skills and experience. Quite possibly the most important piece of the carp fishing jigsaw.

EGG ALBUMEN

Ingredient used in some baits in order to increase a bait's hardness and to slightly alter its consistency.

EGGS

The staple ingredient of most boilies. Eggs are mixed with the base mix and liquid ingredients to form a paste, which is then rolled and boiled, creating a boilie. Some bait makers will leave some of the shell in the mix, as they attempt to create a crunchy texture in their products.

ELSTOW

Famous syndicate of lakes in the Bedford area, run by Linear Fisheries. Elstow One is home to numerous big carp to well over 40lb, with the less densely stocked Elstow Two home to the well-known biggie, The Mother.

ENDURANCE
Sometimes you just have to stick it out for a bite, especially in inclement conditions. Quite often, the worst conditions in terms of our own comfort can be the best conditions in which to catch carp.

END TACKLE
(see terminal tackle)

ENTERPRISE TACKLE *(company)*
Manufacturer of plastic goods, especially noted for its large range of successful imitation hook baits including corn, maggots, pellets, bread, maize, hemp and even water snails.
Website: *www.enterprisetackle.co.uk*

ENTERPRISE TACKLE

ESSENTIAL BAITS *(company)*
Bait manufacturer owned and run by esteemed carp angler and author Mike Willmott. Successful recipes include Essential B5, Creamseed and Bloodworm, each of which has accounted for numerous carp.
Website: *www.essentialbaits.com*

ESSENTIAL OILS
Often also known as 'volatile' or 'ethereal' oils, these are widely used in aromatherapy, but also as bait ingredients. There are literally hundreds, most of which are plant by-products. Examples include geranium oil, garlic oil, black-pepper oil and Mexican onion oil.

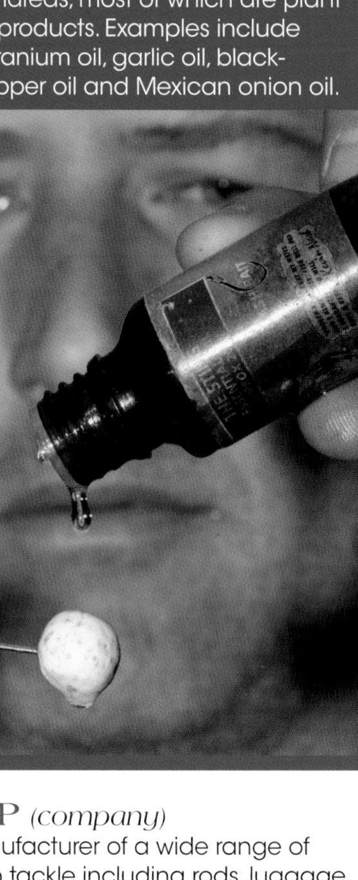

ESP *(company)*
Manufacturer of a wide range of carp tackle including rods, luggage, terminal tackle and PVA.
Website: *www.esp-carpgear.co.uk*

ERICS ANGLING CENTRE *(company)*
Carp tackle shop in Leeds with huge mail-order section and which stocks a huge selection of tackle and bait.
Website: *www.ericsangling.co.uk*

ETIQUETTE
In terms of carp fishing, etiquette is on-the-bank behaviour. You should always be considerate to other anglers on your lake and avoid casting into their water, disturbing their swim or generally causing annoyance to others.

EUROPE

Europe, and European carp fishing, usually refers to the mainland of the Continent. Carp fishing is huge in countries such as the Netherlands, Belgium, France, and Germany and is growing in popularity in eastern European countries too.

Many carp anglers from the UK take fishing trips abroad and the majority of destinations will be in mainland Europe, normally France. Other areas are increasing in popularity.

EYE, THE

Well-known and documented carp that has reached over 50lb in weight and has resided in Sonning Eye lake.

The lake has been developed for watersports as part of the 2012 Olympics and rumours abound of The Eye's demise. As yet this is unproven and, hopefully, she has been moved away from the disturbance and lives happily in some idyllic pond, the location of which shall remain unknown! Former captors include Dave Lane and Chris Pearson.

EXPERIENCE

Can only come with age and time. The more often you go carp fishing, the more experience you gain and, usually, the more efficient an angler you will become.

Experienced anglers make fewer mistakes and are more successful in their decision making. Some noted experienced anglers of the modern age include Dave Lane, Tim Paisley and Ian Chillcott.

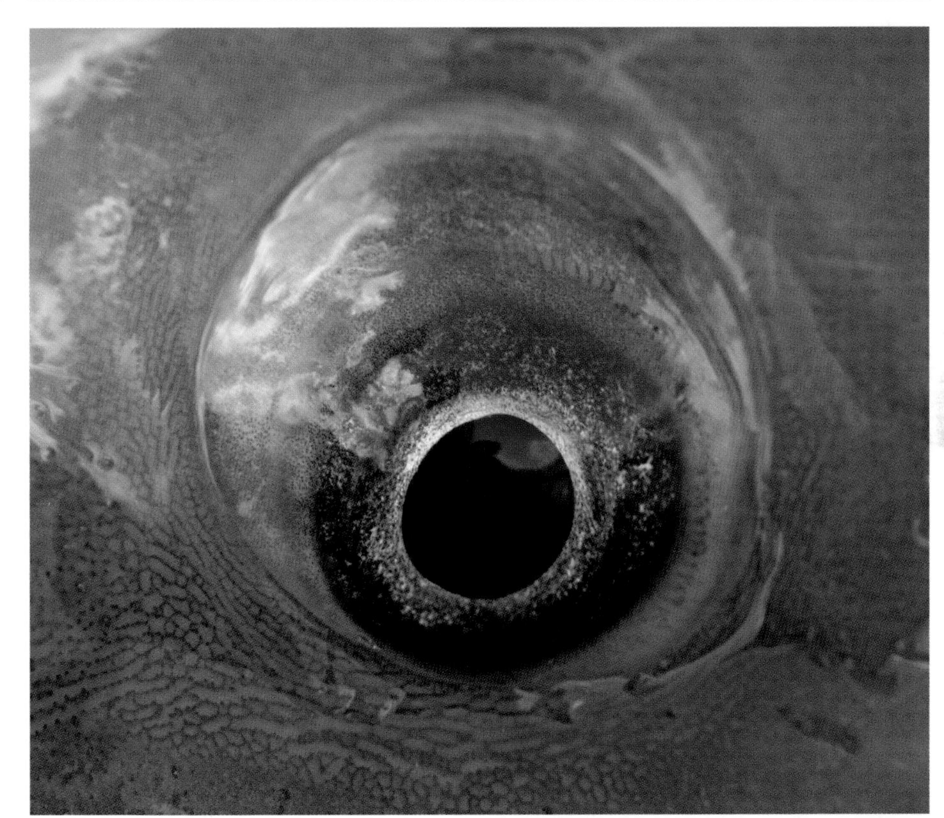

EYESIGHT *(carp and anglers')*

Much is written about what carp can and cannot see, and many theories exist as to the effect this has on our ability to catch them. Although the top scientists can tell us much about this, we do not truly know the exact extent of the carp's visual capabilities.

For anglers, the eyes are a key tool in the carp fishing armoury. Watching the water as much as possible, looking for signs of fish activity and location, will lead to more success.

www.ccmoore.com

BOILIE RANGE
LIVE SYSTEM

QR
NEW
FOX FX
FOX FX
FLATLINER

WE'VE TURNED BEDCHAIR DESIGN UPSIDE DOWN

The revolutionary new FX Flatliner from Fox
takes bedchair design to a whole new level!

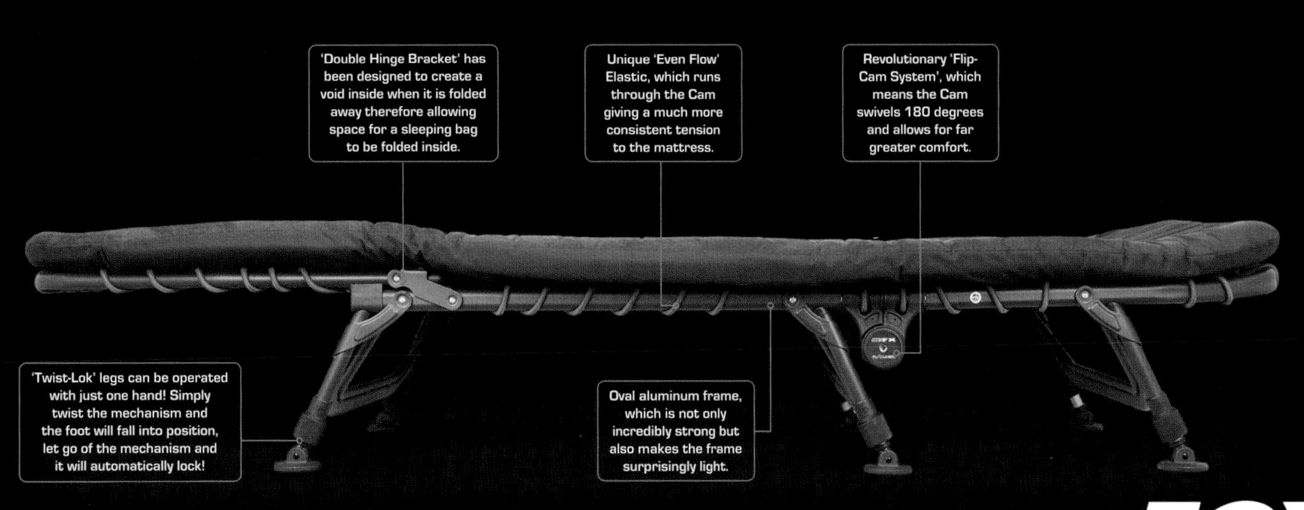
'Double Hinge Bracket' has been designed to create a void inside when it is folded away therefore allowing space for a sleeping bag to be folded inside.
Unique 'Even Flow' Elastic, which runs through the Cam giving a much more consistent tension to the mattress.
Revolutionary 'Flip-Cam System', which means the Cam swivels 180 degrees and allows for far greater comfort.
'Twist-Lok' legs can be operated with just one hand! Simply twist the mechanism and the foot will fall into position, let go of the mechanism and it will automatically lock!
Oval aluminum frame, which is not only incredibly strong but also makes the frame surprisingly light.

FOX
www.foxint.com

Find us on Facebook

FAIRBRASS, DANNY

Leading carp angler and head of carp-tackle manufacturer Korda. As well as launching the Korda brand from scratch, Danny is credited with pioneering the commercial carp fishing DVDs, which now abound. Korda's original Underwater Carp Fishing films were groundbreaking and the template for these has been mimicked ever since.

Dan is also responsible for the capture of many carp of all sizes, and is a keen developer of young carp talent through such schemes as Korda Carp Academy and Carpfest.

FAT LADY, THE

Famous carp which lived in Cambridgeshire's St Ives complex until its death in 2011. With a top weight approaching the magical 60lb barrier, she was one of the largest carp in the UK and many people's PB. The Fat Lady also made up one of the five (at time of writing) UK 50-pounders that Total Carp regular Dave Lane has caught.

FEATURE FINDING

The act of using a lead or a marker setup to locate underwater features and to determine the depth and make-up of the lake.

FEATHERED CAST

When casting a rig out, feathering the cast is an important method that is employed to prevent tangles in the rig and leader. It's done by gently slowing the rate of line leaving the reel just before the lead hits the water, and then trapping the line completely at that moment. This temporarily tightens the line, which forces the rig to straighten so everything lands safely and tangle free.

FINCH, JON

Well-known prolific carp angler and proprietor of Bankside Tackle. Jon is a regular in the pages of Total Carp magazine and is recognised as a master of PVA-bag fishing, although his skills stretch much further than this, both at home and abroad.

FINGERSTALL

Protective sleeve worn on one finger of the top hand when casting. As the angler feathers the cast, the fingerstall protects the finger in question from the abrasion of the line. Particularly important when using braided lines, fingerstalls are essential when spodding and using a marker-float setup for repeated casting. They're usually made from leather, but synthetic versions are also available. Some anglers use a golf glove for similar purposes.

FINS

The protruding parts on the carp's body used for stability, motion and 'steering'. These include the pectoral fins on the fish's underside and the dorsal fin on the back. Combined with the tail (which has an upper and lower lobe or fin) the fins provide the carp with its movement in the water.

FIXED-SPOOL REELS

Reels on which the spool remains motionless while a rotating arm (bail arm) loads the line back on the reel as the handle is turned and line retrieved. Free-spool reels are used almost exclusively in carp fishing, and for the majority of coarse fishing in general.

FISHFINDERS

These are electronic echo sounders that are either integral to or fixed on to boats and bait boats. There are even compact versions available, which can be tied to the line and cast out on to the lake's surface. Fishfinders transmit an electronic 'image' of the underwater depths, features and even location of fish.

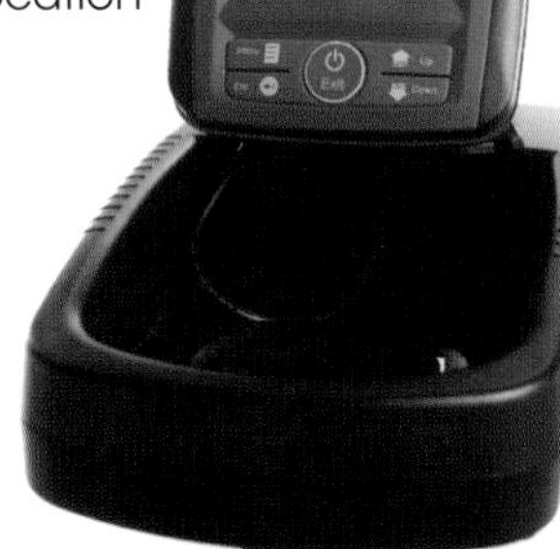

FISHING

See Angling

FIZZING

Colloquial term for the bubbles emerging on the lake surface, particularly when caused by fish feeding on the bottom. The fish that are causing this disturbance are often referred to as 'fizzers'. These are giveaway signs of feeding fish and anglers will often cast their baited rigs to any fizzers they see. They're not always feeding carp, but any fizzers are well worth investigating.

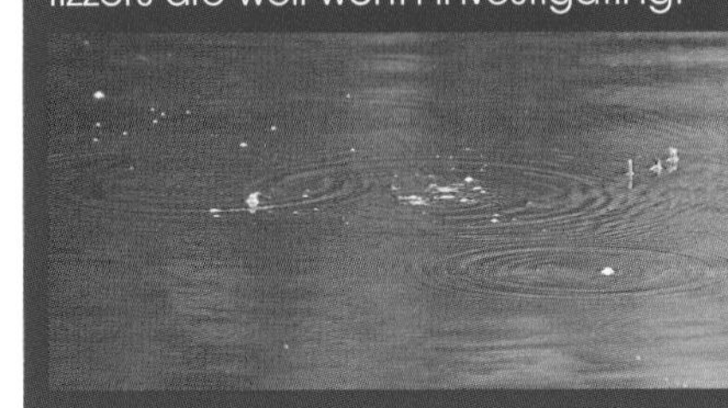

FLAVOURS

There is an array of artificial flavours that are added to baits to increase their attraction. We still do not know exactly how fish 'smell' these baits, but some tend to be more successful than others.

It's often said that many of the flavours available are as much designed to lure anglers into their purchases as they are to entice the carp themselves.

FLEECE
Pilled material used in winter clothing as well as sleeping-bag linings. There are fine-pill, heavy-pill and many variations in between, each suited to different situations and temperatures.

FLOATER FISHING
See Surface Fishing

FLOATERS
Term used to describe the buoyant baits used when surface fishing. Commonly these include mixer biscuits and floating pellets.

FLOAT FISHING
Classic style of fishing, which includes a float that acts as a visual bite indicator and sits on the surface of the lake. There are many types of float available, both small and large, and they are 'cocked' by using a combination of shot which are pinched, at intervals, on the line beneath the float itself.

Dedicated, soft-actioned rods are produced for this style of fishing and tackle normally includes light lines and small hooks for subtle presentations.

FLUORO BAITS
Highly visual baits (usually hook baits) that have near-fluorescent dyes in them to make them stand out. The most popular colours include yellow, orange and pink, and most modern bait companies have some in their range.

FLUOROCARBON

A type of monofilament line, which virtually disappears under water. Fluorocarbon is said to have a refractive index very similar to water and it is this property that helps it become near-invisible when submerged.

Fluorocarbon is widely used as a hook link and leader, and is also becoming increasing popular as a main line. It tends to be stiffer than an equivalent monofilament, and many fluorocarbons also boast excellent abrasion resistance. Regular use of fluorocarbon requires it to be cleaned and maintained for full effectiveness.

FOAM

High-impact, buoyant foam is used in many ways in carp fishing, but most popular is to balance hook baits and use as hook baits in surface and zig fishing. See also Critically Balanced (baits).

FOOD

Don't go fishing without some! Depending on the length of session being fished, the modern carp angler will travel with anything from a flask of soup right through to a large carryall full of ingredients for cooking meals on the bank. Pot Noodles are a firm favourite of many carp anglers, although companies such as Hooked On Foods now produce excellent boil-in-the-bag meals designed to satisfy the session angler's appetite.

FOX, CLIFF

Owner and founder of tackle giant Fox International and inventor of the original angling bedchairs.

FOX INTERNATIONAL

(company)

Multinational, market-leading company in several fields, which manufactures just about every item needed in carp fishing, from bivvies and bedchairs to rods, reels and more.
website: www.foxint.com

FREEBIES

The term used for the loose boilies that are fed into the water, but not attached to a rig. Boilies are despatched using catapults, throwing sticks, spods or by hand and these baits are referred to as the free baits or freebies.

FREE SPIRIT *(company)*
Designer and manufacturer of high-quality carp rods, recognised for its top-end performance and specifications. Website: *www.freespiritfishing.com*

FREE-SPOOL FACILITY
A feature of many modern fixed-spool reels which disengages the 'fixed' spool facility and allows the spool to spin under varying tension when the line is pulled, that is when a carp is hooked and moves off with the baited rig. The most famous version of this is the Baitrunner, which is the patented term to describe the free-spool facility on reels manufactured by Shimano.

FREEZER BAITS
Boilies that are stored in a freezer to maintain their freshness and quality. These boilies are made with eggs and fresh ingredients and, unlike 'shelf-life' boilies, don't contain preservatives, so require storage in sub-zero temperatures to avoid them going 'off'.

FRY
Term used for freshly hatched baby fish and those up to early-infant ages.

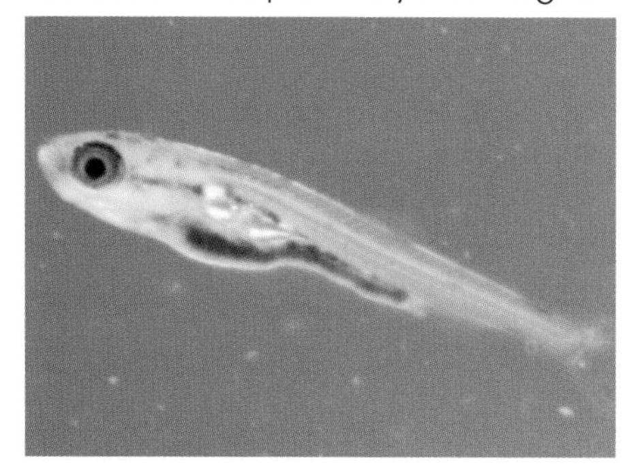

FUJI *(company)*
Multi-national company responsible for the design and manufacturer of hundreds of products. Those products used in carp fishing include market-leading rod rings (guides), reel seats and handles.

Fuji GUIDES®

FULLY SCALED CARP
This term refers to carp that are covered in non-uniform scales but remain categorised as mirror carp and so do not include the more uniformly scaled common carp. Scales on a 'fully' can be small and large or a combination of both.

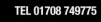

Gg is for...

GARDNER

GARDNER TACKLE

(company)

Tackle company that manufactures and sells a wide range of products including lines, luggage, pods, hooks, terminal tackle and more.
Website: *www.gardnertackle.co.uk*

GET HOOKED ON FISHING

Get Hooked on Fishing

Charity organisation that helps get underprivileged youngsters off the street and into carp fishing.
Website: *www.ghof.org.uk*

GLUGS

Another word used to describe liquid bait dips and soaks.

GOZZERS

Nickname, used mostly by northern match anglers, for maggots.

GRANGE, THE

Classic, original carp bait from the Mainline stable, which dominated waters in its early years and continued to work for many years afterwards. More recently, Mainline has launched its New Grange bait.

GREYS *(company)*

Manufacturer primarily known for its rods (carp, coarse and game), but which also supplies some other complementary carp fishing products, such as waders and clothing.
Website: *www.greysfishing.com*

GAS

Fuel stored in small, portable bottles, which is used to power anglers' stoves. Gas is extremely efficient in most months, but can be a bit unreliable in the winter period when temperatures drop.

Commonly, the gas used by carp anglers is a propane/butane mix and can be bought from tackle shops and outdoor-pursuit retailers.

GOOGLE EARTH ™

Web-based global mapping tool, which is brilliant for locating waters and then inspecting them from an aerial perspective. This is a hugely popular 'tool' for carp anglers.

GRAPEVINE

The community of carp anglers and, specifically, the communication within it. You can pick up information from the carp fishing grapevine and use it to your advantage when targeting certain carp. Internet forums have added to the amount of information and rumour being passed around in recent years.

GRAVEL PITS

When gravel-extrusion companies have finished with a particular site they have a number of options in terms of what to do with it. One of the most environmentally friendly is to fill the excavations with water and landscape them. In fact, this can sometimes be a condition of the original digging contracts being awarded.

Often, and very often back in the 1960s, 1970s and 1980s when the construction of the nation's major motorway and road networks demanded huge quantities of gravel, these are stocked with carp. A significant proportion of the lakes and pits in the UK, which are home to many of the finest carp, are former working gravel pits.

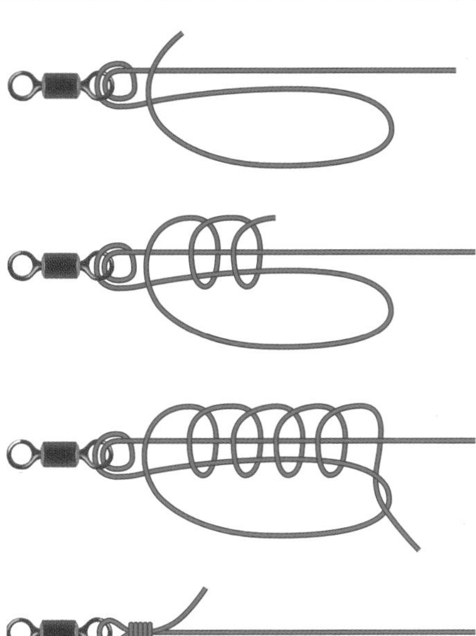

GRINNER KNOT

Popular knot used for attaching swivels to main lines and, in some cases, hooks to rigs. This is a particularly good knot for use with monofilament and fluorocarbon lines, but should always be moistened before it's drawn tight.

GROUNDSHEET

The sheet of material that is laid on the floor prior to erecting a bivvy, creating a barrier between the angler and the ground. They also allow the angler to keep his gear clean when fishing on muddy banks, and they significantly reduce the build-up of condensation.

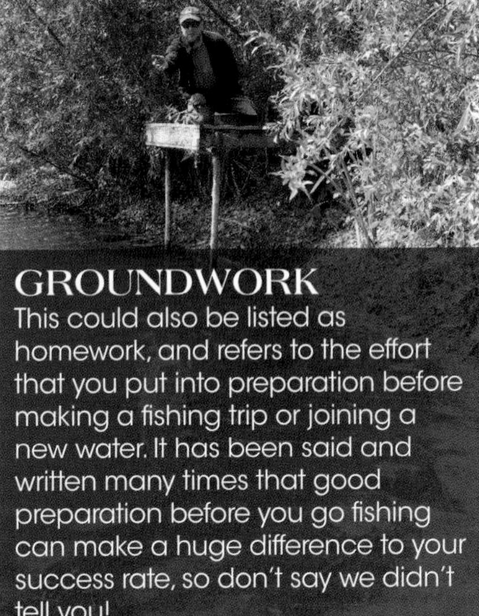

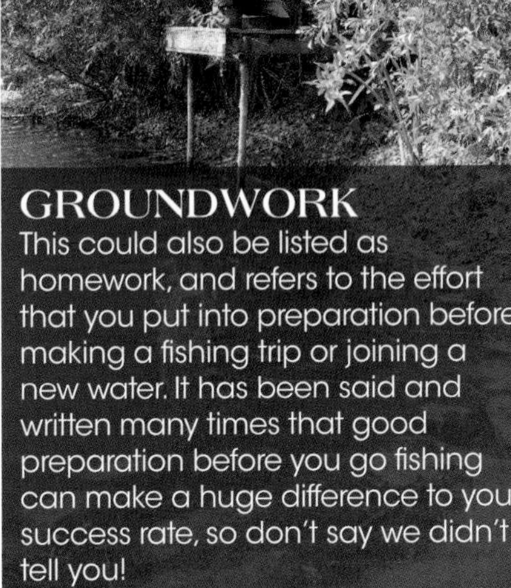

GROUNDWORK

This could also be listed as homework, and refers to the effort that you put into preparation before making a fishing trip or joining a new water. It has been said and written many times that good preparation before you go fishing can make a huge difference to your success rate, so don't say we didn't tell you!

GROWLERS

Nickname for tiger nuts.

GRIPPER LEADS

Although Gripper Leads themselves are a Korda product, the name has become synonymous with the watch lead-type style of weight, as shown in the picture.

Gripper leads are designed primarily for use in running water or on sloping features, as they will stay in position more readily than some other lead designs, especially when used in heavier sizes. Their knobbly design helps them stay put where other leads might roll or slide out of position.

GROUNDBAIT

As the name suggests, this is literally ground-up bait items which are then used as a carpet feed, in a feeder or in PVA bags and sticks. It can also be spodded and used to cloud up the water when fishing zig rigs in mid-water.

There are hundreds of ground-baits available these days and they contain a huge array of ingredients. Many can be bought to match boilie recipes made by several of the major bait manufacturers, and many of the small bait firms too.

If you haven't used groundbait for your carp fishing then give it a go.

GUN, BAIT

In the process of making boilies, the paste mix is placed inside a bait gun and then extruded in long, thin, sausage-shaped lines prior to rolling. These are available in manual versions but there are also larger ones which work with an air compressor, although these tend to be used by rolling companies.

With a big fish spotted, the carp angler
prepares to send out his baited rig...

A B C D E F G H I J K L M N O P Q R S T U V W X Y Z

HAIR RIG

Originally invented by Lenny Middleton/Kevin Maddocks way back in 1980s, the hair was truly revolutionary and can rightly lay claim to making the biggest impact in carp fishing up until then and ever since.

It worked on the principle of separating the hook bait from the hook. So, in the event that the carp attempted to eject the hook bait and rig, the hook remains in the carp's mouth for longer and, so, increases the chances of it nicking the fish and taking hold.

Originally it involved a short piece of supple thread tied to the bend of the hook, and to which the hook bait was threaded or tied. Early users of the hair rig absolutely took places apart and their catch rates were beyond compare.

More recently, the knotless knot has proved the most popular way or tying a hair rig. The majority of modern carp rigs, with some exceptions, however convoluted, generally stick to this principle even today.

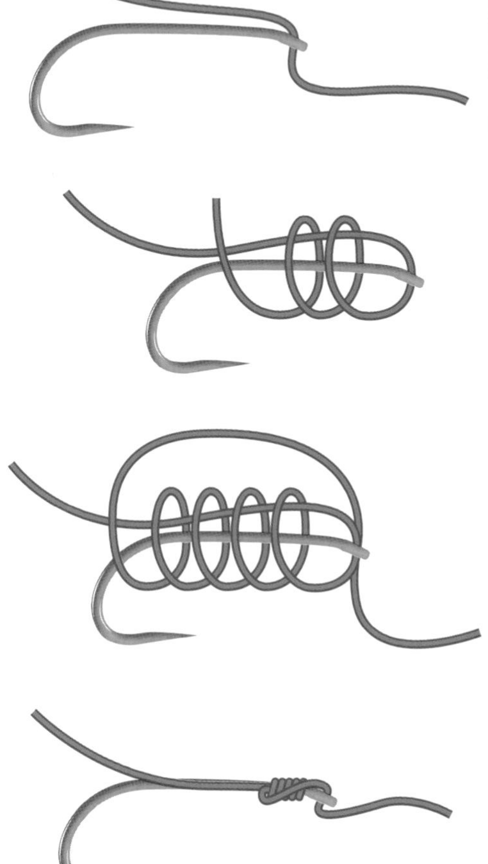

HALIBUT PELLETS

Pellets with an extremely high oil content and adored by carp. There are very many types, in various sizes, available to the modern carp angler.

Due to the high oil content their use should be liberal and not overdone. This also means they are much better suited to use in the warmer months and they are not particularly effective in winter.

HAMIDI, ALI

Well-known carp angler, presenter of the various Korda DVD and TV series, where he is the marketing manager, and author of Carp Fishing Masterclass.

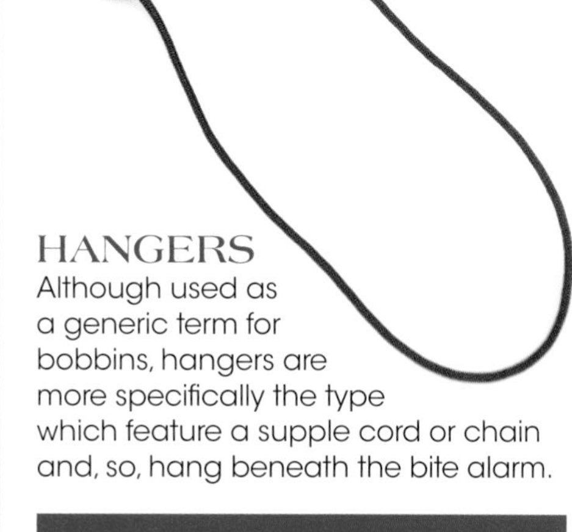

HANGERS

Although used as a generic term for bobbins, hangers are more specifically the type which feature a supple cord or chain and, so, hang beneath the bite alarm.

HARDENED HOOK BAITS

Exactly that, hook baits that have been deliberately made to be much harder than normal. This can be achieved either by the addition of appropriate ingredients at the mixing stage, or by being dried aggressively post rolling.

Hardened hook baits are used to resist the attentions of nuisance species and crayfish, but also by the angler who may want to leave his baits out for excessively long periods.

HARRISON ADVANCED RODS *(company)*

British manufacturer of high-quality carbon products, including bespoke and top-of-the-range carp rods. Popular models include the classic Chimera and modern Torrix, with very many in between.
Website: *www.harrisonrods.co.uk*

Harrison advanced rods

HAULING

Colloquial term for catching a lot of fish in one session or short period. An angler is said to be 'hauling' when enjoying multiple catches regularly.

H BLOCK

High-visibility marker designed to show spots where an angler may be baiting up or fishing. It's shaped like an H and made from hollow, buoyant plastic. Around the inside of the H is wrapped a long line with a large, lead weight at the end. Under no tension, when dropped into a lake from a boat or even bait boat, the lead falls to the lake bed, taking the line with it. The H Block flips over and over but remains on the spot. When the lead hits down the H Block stays put.

HEARN, TERRY

Undoubtedly one of the best carp anglers of his generation, Terry is famous for his ability to catch individual target fish. He is also the author of two books, Still Searching and, previously, In Pursuit Of The Largest, which is widely regarded as one of the best carp fishing books of all time.

HELICOPTER RIGS

Presentation that involves the hook link rotating on the main line or leader, with the lead at the end of this line or leader setup.

When tied correctly, the helicopter rig is, in most cases, the safest rig available to carp anglers. It is important to always ensure that the retaining top bead can slide off the leader and over any knot in the event of the main line breaking, for whatever reason.

HELLEUR, NICK

Prolific carp angler and writer of magazine articles, Nick is a regular in the pages of Total Carp magazine. He is also a true pioneer of foreign waters and has literally thousands of rod hours under his belt and his undoubted talent has seen him catch very many stunning carp from around Europe.

HEMP

Think particle fishing, and you probably conjure up images of hemp and various other seeds. Hemp, however, is undoubtedly the most popular and most effective of them all.

It is harvested from the same plant chain that the illegal substance marijuana emanates, but it is treated so that it cannot be cultivated.

For whatever reason, and the theories range from its oily attractors to its likeness to tiny water snails, hemp is adored by carp and remains one of the very best feed baits available. As with all particles it is important to always soak and then boil hemp correctly, if you are going to prepare your own. However, many companies now sell ready-prepared hemp, which is far more convenient.

HI-ATTRACT BAITS

Generic term for the overflavoured, often brightly coloured, hook baits. These are often used as single hook baits or, with the smaller versions, to tip a normal boilie for added visual and smell attraction.

HOLDALLS

Large bags that are used instead of a rucksack to carry and store the angler's varied items of tackle, clothing, cooking gear and even bait in some instances.

HOOK BAITS

The bait that is actually attached to the rig, and which the angler wishes the carp to find most attractive to the carp. Sinking, buoyant and even critically balanced versions abound and the modern carp angler certainly isn't short of hook-bait choice.

While the large bait manufacturers produce huge quantities of baits, including hook baits, there are companies trading who specialise only in hook baits, which speaks volumes for their popularity.

HOOK

In a nutshell, the small, bent piece of metal with a point at one end, which is used to snare the carp. That's the crude explanation, but in reality modern hooks are designed to be effective, but also kinder to the fish than in days gone by. They come in all manner of patterns and many feature special coatings such as Teflon to aid camouflage and penetration.

Each shape and design of hook is known as a hook pattern, and they vary greatly in manufacturer's ranges.

HOOK-HOLD

When the hook is attached to the carp it is known as the hook-hold. Anglers strive to make the most effective rigs to give a good hook-hold in the correct areas of the mouth, and where the skin is toughest, so the fish is less likely to fall off during the fight.

HOOK-LINK MATERIALS

These are the short sections of line to which the hook is tied and, at the other end a swivel or similar will attach to the main line, leader or lead arrangement.

There are literally hundreds of hook links available to the modern carp angler, but most fall into these three common categories:

Monofilament: Nylon line (see monofilament)

Braided lines: Woven, multi-filament line (see braid)

Coated braids: These are braided lines which have a thin coating, usually a plastic-type material. This coating can be left intact to form a slightly stiffer hook link, or part stripped to form a part-supple and part-stiff 'combi link'.

HOLIDAYS

Specifically, many carp anglers now travel abroad for fishing holidays, in search not only of a good time, but also some very big carp. Many of the carp strains found on mainland Europe can grow to huge proportions, particularly in warmer climes as you go further south. France is undoubtedly the most popular destination, but Holland, Belgium and Spain are also popular. Eastern Europe has a growing reputatation as well. There are many companies now which specialise in carp fishing travel, and an increasing number of venues opening each year to cater for the traveling angler.

HORTON

CEMEX Angling-run water in Surrey which has its place in carp fishing folklore, thanks mainly to some of its famous resident carp, both deceased and alive. Horton's complex features several lakes, the most famous being Church Lake.

ICE

Don't let it put you off going carp fishing, as on well-stocked waters you can still break the ice and create your own spots. Okay, if a lake is completely frozen over then leave well alone, but a bit of cat ice in the margins, or sometimes worse, doesn't always mean the end of your carp fishing.

IMPORTS

Term used to describe carp that are brought into this country from abroad. Illegal imports are those smuggled into the UK and which have great potential to cause harm to UK waters through the spread of diseases that British carp are not equipped to combat.

There is a growing trade in imported carp and the culprits can make significant sums from it. We would plead with lake owners not to buy such fish. If there is no buyer then there is no market and, ultimately, the illegal trade in carp will die.

INLINE LEADS

These are leads with a central bore, through which the main line passes in many presentations. Normally, these will also boast an insert, usually made of plastic or rubber, on to which a tail rubber, or similar, will sit. In some circumstances they can be fished running style, but this is not a particularly common tactic.

INTERNET, THE

The future of all media, not least carp fishing media. We at DHP are constantly striving to bring our readers new web-based material and, in the future, we may all be reading our magazines this way.

The Internet is also the source of almost endless information, which we all plunder to find out about new venues, the weather and so many other things relating to carp fishing, as well as chat to fellow carp anglers on forums and suchlike.

IN-TURNED EYE

This describes the eye of a hook when it is shaped to point slightly inwards, towards the hook point. The angle of this turning in is only slight, but it is widely understood to help the hook and rig's mechanics in many presentations.

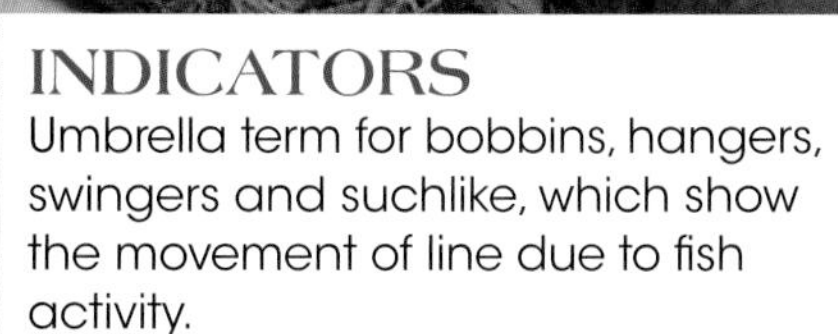

INDICATORS

Umbrella term for bobbins, hangers, swingers and suchlike, which show the movement of line due to fish activity.

ISLANDS

The most obvious features on many carp waters are the islands, and there is good reason for their popularity as a target for anglers. The margins of islands, much as with the lake's margins themselves, are often regular patrol routes for carp and often a bait cast tight to an island margin can be successful.

Islands can often be undercut, which means that the bank beneath the water can be eroded to a level behind the margin itself. This requires an extremely accurate cast to present a baited rig under.

ISOTOPES

Tiny tubes filled with a gaseous material that glows in the dark. They're available in many sizes and colours and are used inside bobbin heads to offer a visual indicator at night.

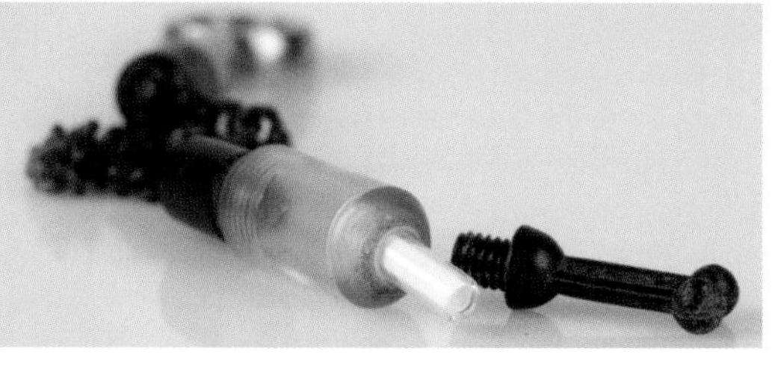

JACKSON, LEE

Former British carp record holder and prolific angler and writer. Lee is one of the most popular anglers on the circuit and, while he does not carp fish quite so regularly these days, he is as gifted a carp angler as there has ever been.

JELLY BAITS

Formerly extremely popular, jelly baits are exactly that. A gelatinous mixture is added to all manner of ingredients to form, literally, a jelly. They are supposed to leak off their attractors quickly and efficiently, but their fall from favour among carp anglers is probably down to their relative ineffectiveness.

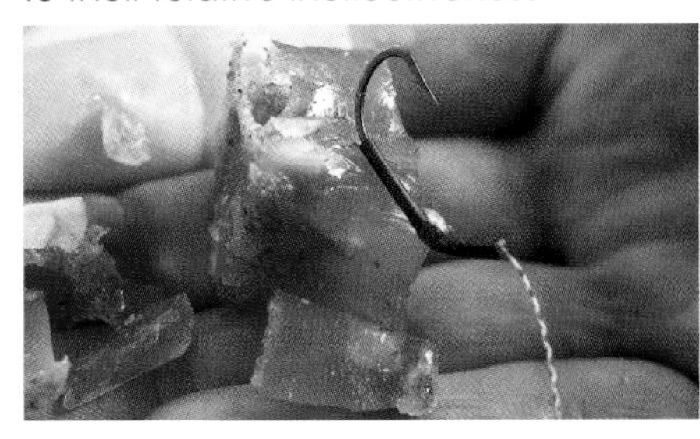

JENKINS, KEITH

Skilled carp catcher, prolific author and writer, and co-founder of the English Carp Heritage Organisation (ECHO).

JRC *(company)*

Manufacturer of a large array of carp tackle, including bedchairs, luggage, rods, terminal tackle, line and clothing. Website: *www.jrc-fishing.com*

JOURNAL

Many anglers keep a journal, or record, of their fishing exploits, and it can be a handy tool in logging your captures and then recalling important information concerning certain angling conditions.

Making a note of temperature, swim location, productive spots, baits and tactics on a given session allows the angler to build up a picture of successful tactics.

KETTLE

Don't go fishing without one! As well as being vital for making the essential cuppa, steam from kettles is also useful in forming certain rigs that incorporate shrink tubing. They can also be used carefully to offer some warmth on those exceptionally cold trips too.

KHV *(Koi Herpes Virus)*

A viral disease that spreads via fish stockings and movement, as well as through flooding from an infected water into a 'clean' one. KHV can devastate the stocks of waters into which it is introduced. Many venues attempt to reduce the risk of KHV and other diseases by insisting on anglers dipping their nets before fishing, or even the compulsory use of the fishery's own nets, slings and mats.

KING CARP

Describes the species of carp for which we go fishing. Mirror, leather and common carp are included in this, but it excludes the 'wild' carp strains.

KNIGHT, KEVIN

Co-proprietor of leading bait company Mainline Baits, hugely talented angler and enthusiastic golfer!

KNOTS

The formation of securing structures in your line to attach hooks and swivels. The ability to tie good, reliable knots is essential to carp anglers. Take the time to learn a few of the more commonly used knots and tie them well. Don't forget to draw knots down gently and to always moisten knots tied in monofilament and fluorocarbon lines before drawing tight.

KORDA *(company)*

One of the most successful carp tackle companies of the 21st century, Korda is known for its array of terminal tackle and, more recently, its groundbreaking DVDs and television programmes.
Website: *www.korda.co.uk*

KRILL

Tiny, plankton-like creatures, similar to microscopic shrimps, which live in huge numbers in the world's oceans. They are rich in vital vitamins and minerals and, when dried, is a popular ingredient in many bait products.

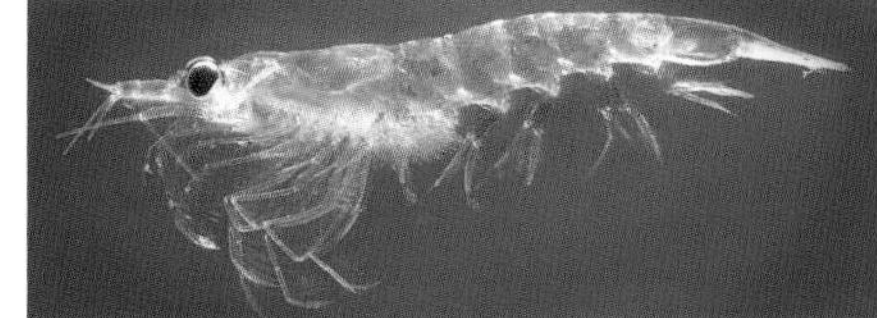

KRYSTON *(company)*

Pioneering carp tackle company, renowned for its hook-link materials. Kryston's Snake-Bite was the first coated braid used by carp anglers.
Website: *www.kryston.com*

L is for...

LAKE

Landlocked area of freshwater, many of which are home to the UK's largest carp. Lakes vary enormously in their make-up, size, shape and depth and this is part of the challenge that appeals to stillwater anglers.

Gravel pits, estate lakes, irrigation pools and ornamental lakes all offer anglers a chance to catch fish, including carp.

LANDING NET

Large net used to safely land a carp that has been played to the bank. Usually featuring a handle of around six feet in length and with a triangular, deep-meshed net at the end, they're available from most tackle manufacturers in all manner of styles and to suit every budget.

Never go carp fishing without an ample landing net, capable of safely holding the biggest fish you might be likely to encounter. It's a very good tip to carry two landing nets, as you could well experience a double bite and be in a bit of a pickle if you only have one net with you.

LANE, DAVE

Pound for pound Dave Lane is possibly the greatest carp angler of his generation and has accounted for very many of the UK's biggest and best-loved carp. When asked who is the most impressive angler he has ever worked with, editor of Total Carp magazine Marc Coulson often cites Dave as being that man. Hugely talented, hard working and, even as he approaches his latter years (!), Dave is still extremely motivated to catch carp, and that pretty much covers the three key ingredients of what makes the best anglers.

LEAD

A weight that is used to provide both casting weight and an anchor against which the fish is hooked.

There is a huge array of lead styles available to the modern carp angler, many of which are covered elsewhere in this book, and they come in a great many shapes and sizes. Each of these is designed with a specific purpose in mind.

There are several weights on the market made from non-lead materials, but these still tend to be referred to colloquially as 'leads' nonetheless.

LEAD CLIP

Small tackle item that retains the lead during casting, but is capable of releasing the lead under tension. This is done for the safety of the fish and to increase the angler's chances of landing a hooked carp. For example, if a fish charges into heavy weed the lead can become a dangerous obstacle, but the lead clip allows its release and so reduces the risk of tethering and suchlike.

Lead clips are a very good example of how carp anglers have evolved their tackle with the utmost priority being carp welfare and safety.

LEADCORE

This leader material is constructed from a lead-wire inner and a braided, hollow outer material. The lead can be removed from inside and the material then spliced into loops and knots to allow its attachment to swivels and main lines. Due to its construction, leadcore sinks extremely quickly and is therefore used to pin the end tackle to the lake bed and away from carp's fins.

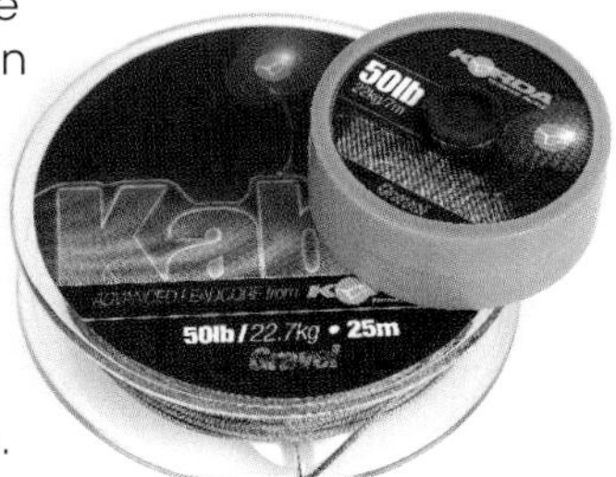

LEADER

A material used between the lead and the main line, usually to either pin the line down (see Leadcore) or to cope with the strain of strong casts with large leads. In the case of the latter, they are known as casting leaders and are often made from high breaking strain mono or braided lines.

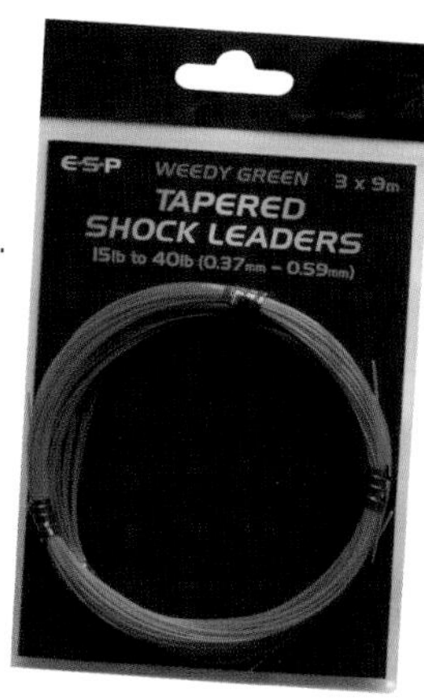

LEADER KNOTS

The knots used to attach leaders to the main line. It is vital when tying a leader knot that it is secure and that it passes safely through the rod rings.

It is also absolutely essential that any items being used on the line can pass safely over this leader knot. This includes inline leads, sleeves, beads and similar items. Many venues ban the use of leaders as they prefer not to take the risk of anglers using them incorrectly.

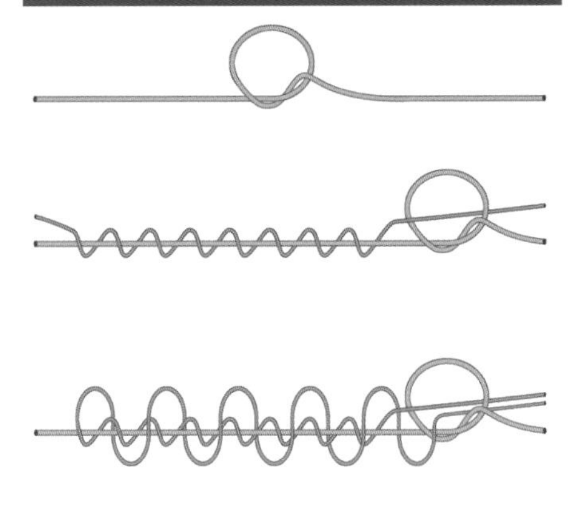

LEATHER CARP

A variety (we hesitate to use the word 'strain') of carp that features no scales on its body. Some anglers refer to carp with just a small scale or two near its tail, underside or fins as leathers, but a true leather has no scales at all. The fins on a true leather carp are said to 'melt' into the fish's body. True leather carp are comparatively rare, and the most famous example is Yateley's Heather, a much-written-about carp and a target for some of the most famous anglers of the modern era.

LED

This stands for light-emitting diode and it has many applications in modern lighting. The most common use in carp fishing is in the heads of bite alarms. LEDs are activated when the line moves across the sensor of an alarm, and they come in many different colours.

LEECHES

Leeches are parasitic, worm-like creatures that occur naturally all over the world and feed on the blood of a host animal. A tiny variety of leech frequents nearly every stillwater in the country and they often attach themselves to carp, particularly in the winter when carp will often lie dormant for long periods. Anglers often mistake leech presence as a sign of poor health in carp, but they are just part of the ecological make-up of the lake and do the fish relatively little harm at all.

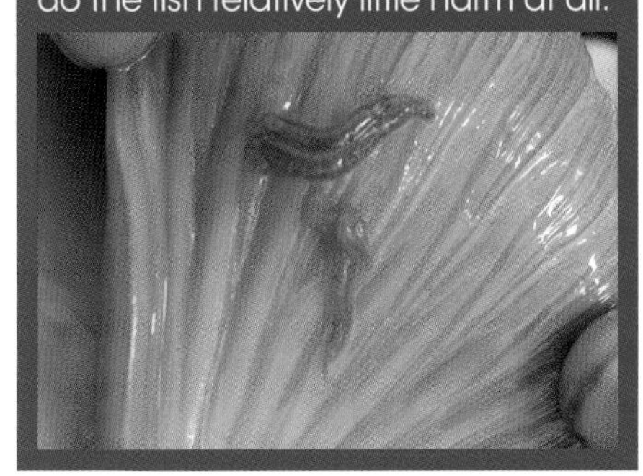

LINEAR CARP

Another variety of carp, this time included in the mirror carp category and which features a row, or rows, of scales along the length of its flank.

LINEAR FISHERIES

One of the most popular day-ticket venues in the UK, Linear Fisheries' main Oxfordshire site boasts multiple lakes including St John's, Oxlease, Manor Farm, Hardwick and Hunt's Corner. These waters are home to a large number of big carp, many of which are beautiful specimens of the species.

Head bailiff Roy Parsons is a living legend among the carp angling fraternity and he and Linear Fisheries have seen many of the country's top carp anglers account for its famous fish.

LEEWARD BANK

This refers to the bank of the lake that sits at the 'back' of the wind. In other words it is the bank from which direction the wind blows, as opposed to the bank that the wind blows into. The water nearest the leeward bank is said to be in 'the lee' of the wind and carp will often favour this area in the event of prolonged cold winds, especially in winter.

LIQUIDS

In the carp fishing sense these are liquid additives that are included in boilie mixes or which are added to groundbaits or used as dips and so on. Oil-based liquids can be used in PVA products, but all water-based liquids should be dried off if the baits they are added to are to be used in PVA bags.

LOBWORMS

Not so popular with modern carp anglers, although 'lobs' are still a hugely effective carp bait. Worms, particularly big fat juicy ones, are packed full of amino acids that the carp adore. Chopped worms in conjunction with a dry groundbait make a great PVA bag filling, and two halves of lobworm are a superb stalking bait for carp in the margins.

LUGGAGE

The general term for 'soft' goods such as rod holdalls, carryalls, rucksacks and suchlike. Most carp luggage is olive green or 'camou' and there are literally hundreds of types on the market these days, from a plethora of manufacturers.

THE UK'S NUMBER ONE BIG-CARP MAGAZINE ON YOUR iPHONE OR iPAD

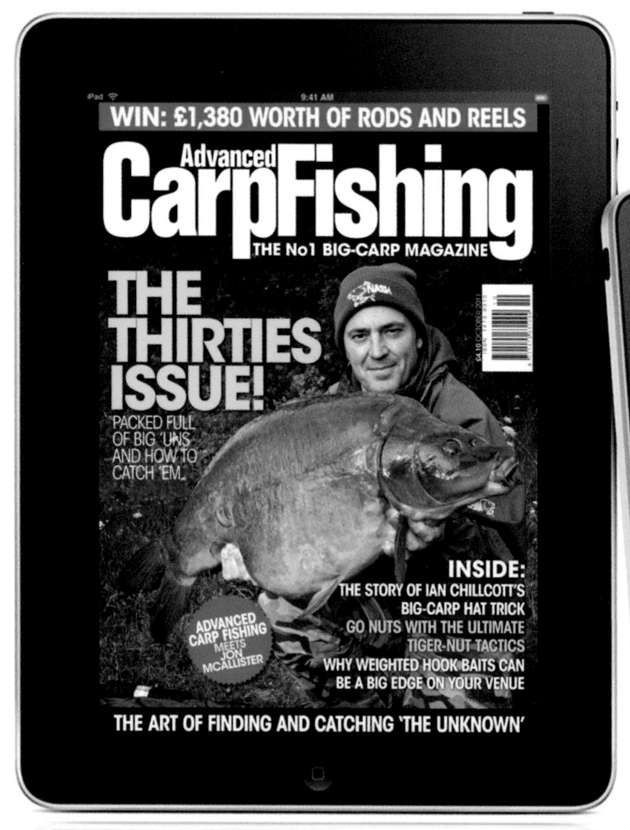

OUT NOW!

(ALL THE FEATURES, NO PAPER CUTS)

SEARCH 'ADVANCED CARP FISHING'

WE'RE LIVE ON THE ANDROID MARKET TOO!

PLUS! ALL THESE GREAT FISHING TITLES ARE ALSO AVAILABLE ON iTUNES & ANDROID

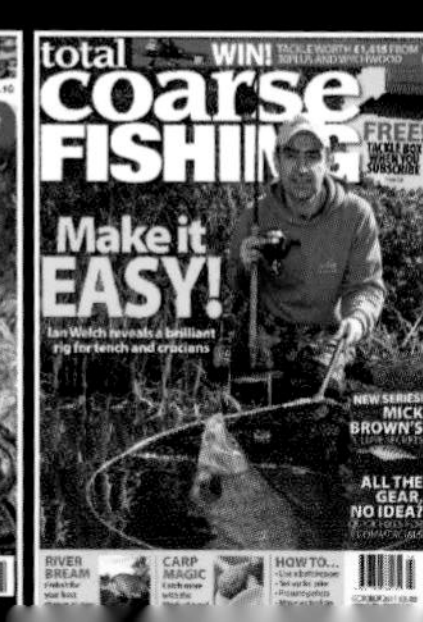

Mm is for...

MACMILLAN, IAIN
Well-known carp angler and regular in just about every carp magazine on the planet! Iain hails from Staffordshire but has made a name for himself catching carp from all manner of waters much farther afield.

MAG-ALIGNER
This rig is a version of the line-aligner, and was invented by carp angling master Rob Maylin. Rob replaced the shrink tubing on the line-aligner with an imitation maggot and the rig was a revelation. It has been refined ever since and continues to be the rig of choice for anglers fishing with maggots. It's usually used in conjunction with a mesh-type PVA bag of maggots, but can feasibly be used in many situations.

MAGAZINES
There are myriad carp fishing magazines out there these days with the biggest selling being Total Carp, which at the time of going to print sells in excess of 23,000 copies every month in the UK.

Total Carp's sister magazine, Advanced Carp Fishing, is the number-one specimen carp angler's read, with sales figures around 16,000.

These magazines are a valuable source of information for the modern carp angler, and provide up-to-date tips and tactics on how to improve your catch rate, whatever the size of your intended quarry.

MAGGOTS
The grubs of the bluebottle fly, maggots have been a popular angling bait for centuries. There are very few freshwater fish that will not eat maggots and that includes carp… big time!

These days maggots are available in several colours (they're dyed by breeders impregnating their food with colourings), but reds and whites are by far the most effective for carp.

MAIN LINE

This refers to the line loaded on to the spool of the angler's reel and which provides the link between the reel and the lead system or rig. Usually, carp anglers use monofilament lines of between 8lb and 15lb breaking strain.

MAINLINE BAITS

(company)

Essex-based bait giant, responsible for several of the most popular carp baits of all time, including The Cell. Website: *www.mainline-baits.com*

MAIZE

Large kernel, similar to giant sweetcorn, but from the maize plant. Some anglers rate this highly as a carp bait, but then there are many others who think it has had its day.

Still popular with anglers travelling abroad (it's cheap and can be stored easily once prepared) it does little in terms of nutrition, although can be used as roughage in complementing a diet of higher-protein food.

MAKER, TOM

Young carp angler who is hugely gifted and widely tipped to be one of the future carp fishing superstars. Tom is already a prolific catcher of big carp and, for one so young, possesses the skill and knowledge of one much older.

MARGINS

Refers to the area of water closest to the banks, on the near or far side and including islands. Although many anglers neglect them in favour of long-range fishing, the margins are often the single best feature on any lake.

Fish love to patrol margins of lakes in search of food, both the natural variety and that which has been thrown in by anglers. This is especially true on commercial waters, which see anglers discard unwanted bait in the margins after their regular matches. Carp, and often the bigger carp in the lake, can regularly be seen mopping up this bait after matches have taken place.

If you are ever in any doubt as to where to fish on a new venue, always check out the margins. Wandering round and baiting a few margin spots, then returning later with a baited rig, is a wonderfully effective and exciting, method of carp fishing.

MARKER FLOAT

The float used in the marker setup, along with marker rod and lead, to plumb the depths of lakes.

The angler casts out the marker setup, winds the line down tight to the lead and then lets line slowly off the reel, one foot at a time. When the float hits the surface, the number of times the line has been 'paid out' signifies the approximate depth of the lake. The float gives the element of buoyancy to bring the line up, and also the visual element once it pops to the surface.

Marker floats can then be left out in the lake while bait is spodded out, before being wound back in and used all over again on a different spot.

The skilled feature finder will not only ascertain depths but will drag the marker float and, specifically, the lead to 'feel' the make-up and contours of the lake bed. This requires practice, but once mastered can be a hugely significant element in the carp angler's armoury.

MARKER KNOT

Using a braided material, power gum or even elastic, these are tied to the main line to provide a semi-permanent marker on the line so that the angler can make repeated, accurate casts.

Once a rig has been cast out, the line is gently tightened down to the lead. The marker knot is then tied to the line somewhere in the region of the reel, or just off the rod tip. After playing a fish, the line is then cast back out and retrieved until the marker knot returns to its original position. The line can then be placed in the line clip on the reel, wound back in and recast accurately to the same spot. The cast needs to be feathered just before the line hits the clip so as to avoid cracking off or damaging the line itself. Once finished with, the marker knot can be pulled or carefully snipped off.

Snapshot of a marker knot

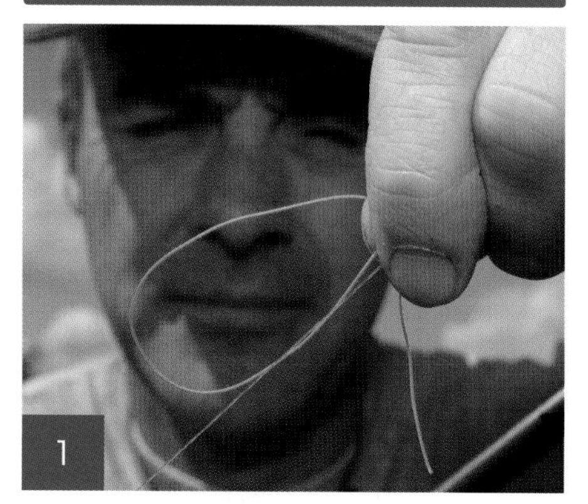

Form a loop of marker braid or pole elastic alongside your main line.

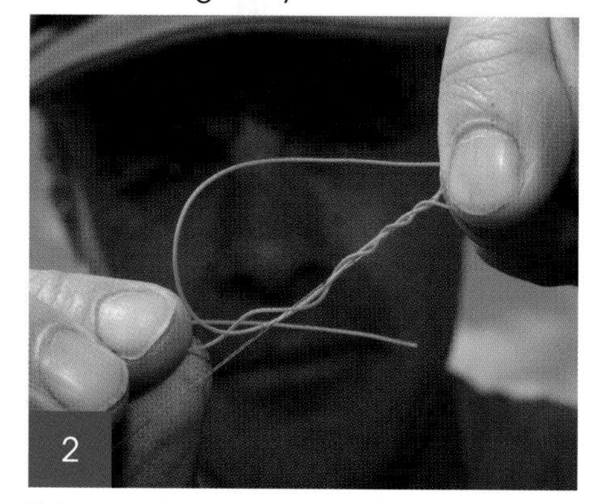

Take one tag end through the loop and over your main line five times.

Moisten the marker material and gently pull on both tags to draw tight.

MARKER ROD

The rod used for feature finding, in conjunction with the marker float and setup. Usually features a test curve of around 3lb, but some long-range versions may differ.

Ideally, the best marker rods should have a fairly stiff tip section, contrary to some popular belief and very many previous models from some manufacturers.

When dragging the lead around to feel the make-up of the lake bed, the 'bumps' and 'knocks' are transmitted back through the rod tip to the angler. Marker rods are best coupled with braided main lines as these near-zero-stretch lines offer the maximum in sensitivity when feature finding.

MARY

Although perhaps not as renowned among the latest generation of carp anglers, Mary is one of the most famous carp that has ever swum in the UK. Formerly the British record carp at well over 50lb, Mary resided in the equally famous Wraysbury One before her natural demise. Well-known captors include Terry Hearn and Dave Lane, the two most gifted anglers of the modern era.

MARUKYU *(company)*

Japanese bait manufacturer that has recently emerged in the UK market. Its products are based on intensive scientific knowledge and experimental testing and the ingredients are all naturally occurring aquatic materials. Website: *www.marukyu.co.uk*

MARUKYU

MATCH-CARP FISHING

Increasingly popular morphing of carp angling and match fishing, carp matches are typically held over a 48-hour period and usually consist of teams, of two anglers, competing against each other.

There are some very big prizes available these days and there is even an official World Carp Fishing Championship. Matches require absolute effort and dedication and competitors – the better ones at least – tend to get very little sleep through the duration of a match.

MAYLIN, ROB

Although an overused term, Rob is truly one of carp fishing's living legends. His writing took carp fishing to a new audience, he continues to write exceptionally and his record in terms of carp catches is almost beyond compare.

MIDDLETON, LENNY

Taxidermist and carp angler, Lenny is widely credited with the invention of the hair rig and his name will always be synonymous with carp fishing.

MILKY

Nickname for well-known, and hugely gifted, carp angler and all-round top bloke Gary Lowe.

MILK PROTEINS

The majority of milk proteins are not simply found in milk but are actually unique to milk. Milk proteins are packed with natural amino compounds which aid in growth. In carp fishing, several milk proteins – the most common being the caseins – are used as base ingredients to boilies, and provide excellent dietary supplements for the carp.

MIRROR CARP

Unlike the common carp, which is covered in uniform rows of similar scales, the mirror carp is a variety of king carp featuring random scale patterns that do not usually cover the carp's flanks.

Biologically the mirror and common carp are the same, but genetically there are subtle differences. Although originally bred selectively by monks (they found the fewer scales easier to remove prior to cooking) these differences now prohibit the mirror from one day evolving back into the common variety.

One aspect of this irregular scale patterning is that each mirror carp is unique and, as such, easily recognisable. This is especially true as they grow bigger although, sadly, by then they will normally have acquired nicknames!

MOBILITY

Often vital to the catch rate of anglers, the ability to stay mobile is a string to the successful carp angler's bow. Sightings of carp in a different area of the lake, a change of weather conditions or even the forecast of a change in conditions can all lead the angler to want to move swims to stay in contact with the fish. This is especially the case on larger venues.

In order to do this, many anglers travel light and take only the essentials. This makes it quick and relatively easy for them to pack away and move at a moment's notice. An angler who is bivvied up in a swim, and surrounded by barrow loads of gear is far less likely to move than the mobile angler and, so, will often miss opportunities as a result.

MOLASSES

Sticky and super sweet in nature, molasses is a bi-product of maize processing and is sold all over the world as an animal feed supplement. It has long been used in carp fishing as an additive to groundbait mixes and suchlike, but be warned – bream also find it extremely attractive!

MONOFILAMENT

Also referred to as nylon, but not always strictly speaking made of such, monofilament line (mono) is a continuous line extruded at different thicknesses, and therefore breaking strains, from a single fibre of a plastic-type material. Mono is by far the most popular line used in carp fishing, or most fishing for that matter, and is available in numerous breaking strains and colours. The colour element is usually from a dye added before extrusion, and many believe that such coloured lines are less strong than 'clear' versions.

MOON PHASES

The moon undoubtedly has a huge effect on all of nature, the world over, and it is widely accepted that the different phases of the moon represent differing levels of success when carp fishing, as they have an impact on the behaviour of the carp.

There is still some conjecture as to exactly how this prevails, but one thing that many carp anglers agree on is the 'new moon' is almost certainly the best time to target carp, especially big ones.

MONUMENT, THE

Day-ticket carp lake near Shifnal, in Shropshire, which is well known for its stock of enormous carp. While there are plenty of carp in this size bracket across the UK, seldom are they found in such numbers in a day-ticket venue. Owned and run by Rob Hales, The Monument is open to all, but must be pre-booked.

MOZZIES

Abbreviation of mosquitoes, the blood-sucking beasties that often live in boggy areas and near to water, and which represent a real nuisance to the carp angler.

MUSSELS

Variety of clam-like mollusc, mussels are often found in freshwaters, sometimes in huge numbers. The most common freshwater mussels that carp anglers encounter are pea mussels and zebra mussels. These can fray lines with their sharp-edged shells, especially in large colonies, and they can even clamp on to anglers' baits or rigs on occasion.

Some saltwater mussel species are also used as bait ingredients and additives, the most popular being the New Zealand green-lipped mussel, which is recognised as a brilliant boilie ingredient.

As night-time descends,
so too does the feeling of anticipation...

A B C D E F G H I J K L M N O P Q R S T U V W X Y Z

RP PRODUCTS

OP-UPS AND OTHER MUST-HAVE BAIT PRODUCTS

BOILIE RANGES

INCLUDES A HOOKBAIT DIP, LIQUID ATTRACTANT AND 15MM & 20MM POP-UPS

Spicy Peanut

- Made using a nut flour base mix with added crushed peanuts
- Contains red chilli flakes to stimulate a Carp's taste
- With added peanut oil, designed to attract Carp onto the bait

White Chocolate

- Contains real white chocolate and ground coconut - proves irresistible to Carp
- Highly visible white colour making it easy for Carp to locate

Green Lipped Mussel Boilie Range

- Made using a high protein fishmeal base mix
- Includes the finest quality Green Lipped Mussel from New Zealand – the top proven fish attractor

To find out more go to our new website: **www.DYNAMITEBAITS.com**

Nn is for...

NASH, KEVIN

Hugely successful and respected carp angler, and developer of a myriad of carp products, rigs and methods. Kevin has been around forever, seemingly, and was a true pioneer of carp fishing in his earlier years. More recently he has caught the biggest brace of carp from the UK and continues to pursue, and catch, huge and magnificent carp. Kevin is also the proprietor of Nash plc.

NASH plc *(company)*

Essex-based tackle and bait giant, which manufactures and sells everything from bedchairs, bivvies, sleeping bags and boilies, to terminal tackle, PVA, luggage and clothing.
Website: *www.nashtackle.com*

NATURALS

The term to describe any natural food that carp eat, either in their normal environment or when introduced by anglers. It's a widely used term and covers everything from bloodworm, snails and caddis-fly larvae, which all occur naturally in lakes and water systems, to maggots, worms and casters that are less prevalent naturally but which anglers make prolific use of. Maggots in particular are a popular carp bait and have enjoyed a renaissance in recent years, accounting for huge numbers of carp.

NEEDLES

As in baiting needles. These are used to thread baits on to hairs and suchlike or, in the case of stringer needles, for threading boilies on to PVA tape or string. There are several needle designs available these days, some of which have been deliberately designed to make them easy to extract from fingers in the event of all-too-common accidents!

NEOPRENE

Robust, waterproof and flexible synthetic material used in the manufacture of waders and boots. Neoprene, unlike rubber or nylon, also offers an insulating layer when wading in cold water.

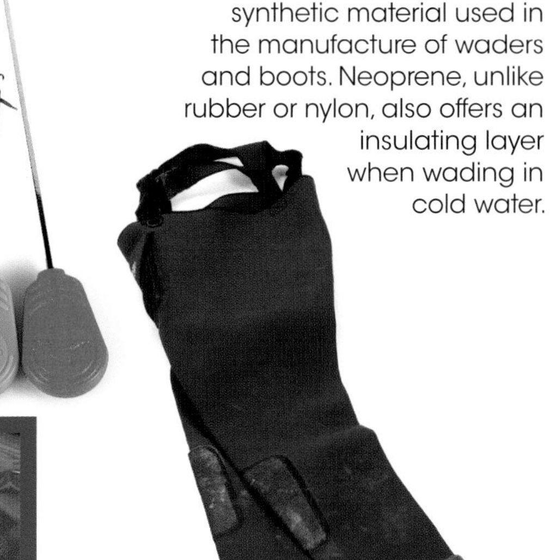

N-BUTYRIC ACID

Incredibly potent and effective bait additive that is used in very small doses in many hi-attract hook baits. Be warned if using this stuff, it absolutely stinks! No wonder that one of the biggest suppliers of N-Butyric in the carp market, Nutrabaits, supplies it in a sealed bag within a tightly closed plastic tub.

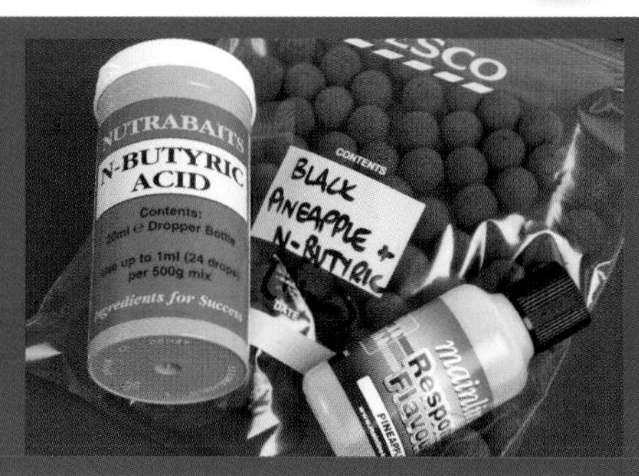

NETTINGS

Lake owners will often enlist the help of members or staff to run large nets through the lake for a number of reasons. These include fish census, removal of certain species and for the selling on of resident fish.

NIGHT FISHING

Many carp anglers, and other specimen anglers, will fish into and through the night. There are a number of specialist items of equipment required, including bivvy and bedchair, as well as head torch, stove and more. Night fishing is extremely popular and many anglers will fish for at least 24 hours on many of their trips.

NODDIES

Term rather cruelly used to describe incapable anglers on the bank. Wrongly, this is also sometimes used to poke fun at beginners and novice anglers, often by small-minded individuals with minimal social skills!

NUISANCE SPECIES

Generic term to describe any species, not targeted by the carp angler, which in some way makes carp fishing more difficult. While it includes birds and crayfish, more usually it refers to other species of fish, such as bream, tench and roach. These fish can often be caught on carp baits, despite not being the intended quarry and so are deemed to cause a 'nuisance' to carp anglers.

NUTS

There are several nuts that are used as effective carp baits, the most common being tiger nuts. Brazils and hazelnuts are also exceptional hook baits and peanuts have long been thought of as one of the best baits around.

It is important – vital in fact – to prepare nuts properly, as it is with any 'particle' bait. Sufficient soaking (at least 24 hours normally) and boiling (this varies with the nut) are needed in order to ensure that the nut is safe to use. Failure to do this can see nuts swell in size once introduced to the water. If this swelling occurs in the fish's gut then it can cause digestive problems.

Many fisheries, a majority in fact, actually ban the use of nuts these days as they do not want to take the risk of anglers using nuts which have not been properly prepared for fishing. Some fisheries allow the use of pre-prepared nuts in jars, as sold by a variety of bait companies, but these are in the minority.

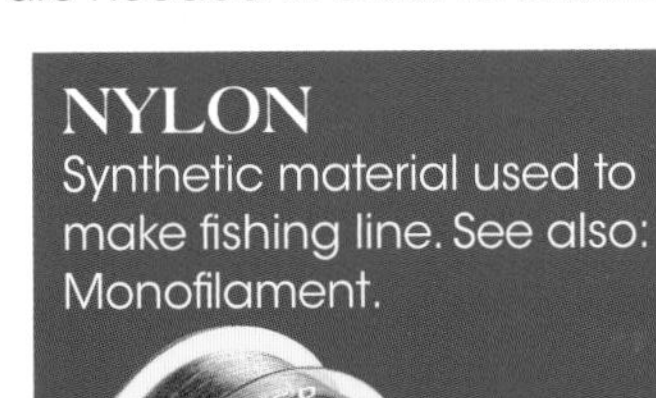

NYLON

Synthetic material used to make fishing line. See also: Monofilament.

A B C D E F G H I J K L M N O P Q R S T U V W X Y Z

Oo is for...

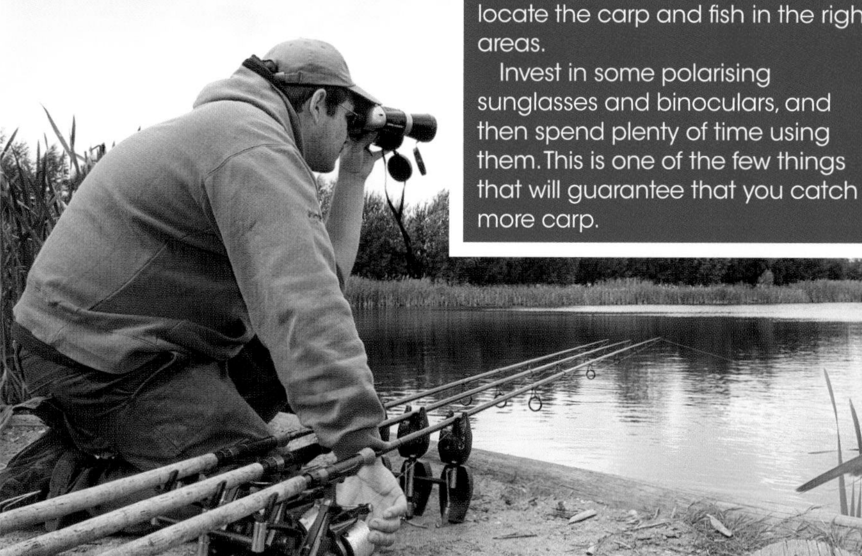

OBSERVATION

Watching the water is an essential aspect of carp fishing. An hour spent observing the lake, looking for signs of carp activity and location, is worth five hours' fishing. Location is everything in carp fishing and watching the lake will help you locate the carp and fish in the right areas.

Invest in some polarising sunglasses and binoculars, and then spend plenty of time using them. This is one of the few things that will guarantee that you catch more carp.

OPTONICS

A brand of early bite alarms, which also became a generic term for buzzers for some time. More recently, Optonics have been re-born under the Sundridge banner and the newer models are much more advanced, and reliable, compared to their predecessors.

ODOURS

Every one of us has an individual body odour, and it has been said and written many times that some people's natural odour can be a fish repellent. It follows that some people might be blessed with a more neutral odour and, you never know, some of us may even be lucky enough to give off smells that carp like. The carp's sense of smell is far greater than ours so they can pick up even the slightest odour. Avoid washing your hands or dishes with soap and then touching your rigs and baits. Many anglers believe in rinsing their hands in lake water on a regular basis in order to mask any odours on their hands.

The jury is out in terms of cigarette odours on smokers' fingers, but with very many of the big-name carp anglers being smokers it's difficult to suggest that carp are turned off by this. One to definitely watch out for is synthetic grease or oil on fishery padlocks, and definitely wear a glove if you fill your car with petrol on the way to the lake.

OILS

Very many oils are used as bait ingredients and additives to boilie mixes and suchlike. They are also widely used to add a moist element to PVA bag and stick mixes and, vitally, they do not melt PVA products.

There are several extremely popular oils, including salmon oil and hemp oil, as well as several nut oils. It's important that, while these oils are excellent additives, you should never overdo their use. It's especially important to not use too much oil in colder water conditions, as oils congeal below a certain temperature and lose their effectiveness. They're also not so easily digested by carp in this form and when the carp's metabolism is slowed by cooler conditions.

OKUMA *(company)*

Manufacturer of top-quality fishing reels, including several models intended for carp fishing, many with freespool facility. Website: *www.okumafishingteam.com*

OTTERS

Often quoted as the second most protected species worldwide, (behind dolphins) otters have made a comeback in the UK over recent years. Thanks in no small part to the Tarka series of books and TV programmes, as well as their cuddly appearance, otters are extremely popular with naturalists and very many have been re-introduced to UK water systems.

In fact, in mid-2011, the otter was officially listed as now inhabiting every county of England. This is all well and good from the environmentalists' perspective, but irresponsible re-introductions have led, in some areas, to an overpopulation of otters, which in turn has seen them devastate fish stocks in many rivers. They have then turned their attentions to stillwaters, often stocked at costs of thousands of pounds, and now the otter is a very real and present danger to commercial fisheries the country over.

It costs a huge amount of money for fisheries to protect themselves, often by electric perimeter fencing, but many face this or the depletion of their stocks.

It's a terrible example of an environmental situation that, at first glance, appears like a success story, but the indigenous fish of the UK's rivers and lakes are suffering hugely as a result.

OUT OF BOUNDS

An area of a lake where no fishing is allowed. Usually, this means a bank of the lake where anglers are not allowed to fish from, but can cast towards from other areas of the same venue. Sometimes, however, it will mean an entire section of the lake itself in which angling is not allowed.

OUT-TURNED EYE

This refers to the pattern of hook where the eye (the loop at the end of the shank) is angled away from the point. Essentially, the opposite of the in-turned eye earlier on in this encyclopaedia.

The reason for this eye is that it suits the use of stiff monofilament lines used in the creation of chod rigs, stiff rigs and suchlike. The eye helps maintain the correct angle of line, where an in-turned eye would not. As a result, hooks with out-turned eyes are often referred to as 'stiff-rig hooks'.

OVAL BROLLY

Umbrellas were the shelter of choice for carp anglers for many years and, at some point, extra sections of material were added to create side panels for extra protection. The design then went a step further with the brolly body being made more oval in shape and the rear sections of material reaching all the way to the ground, via extended rear spines. These became known as oval brollies and are pretty much the same design today.

OVERNIGHTERS

This is the term referring to a fishing session that only lasts for one night. Often, it will involve an angler going fishing after work, fishing through the night and then getting up and returning to work the next day.

OVERHAND KNOT

The simplest knot to tie, and one that many people know as a granny knot. Although not used to tie hooks or swivels and suchlike to line, as it does not hold sufficient strength, it does have some uses in carp fishing, such as finishing off a loop of bait floss.

OVERWRAP

A large, additional section of material that can be added to a bivvy or umbrella to form a second skin. It is literally wrapped over the shelter and then pegged down, hence the name overwrap. Most modern bivvies these days have a matching wrap, or skin, available.

These wraps are designed to trap a layer of warmer air between it and the bivvy and, so, they add insulation and reduce condensation within the bivvy itself in winter. Often, as in the picture, the outer skin can freeze up, but the bivvy inside remains insulated and makes the angler much more comfortable.

Pp is for...

PALOMAR

A type of knot used commonly by carp anglers to tie line to swivels, rings and sometimes hooks, depending on the rig in use.

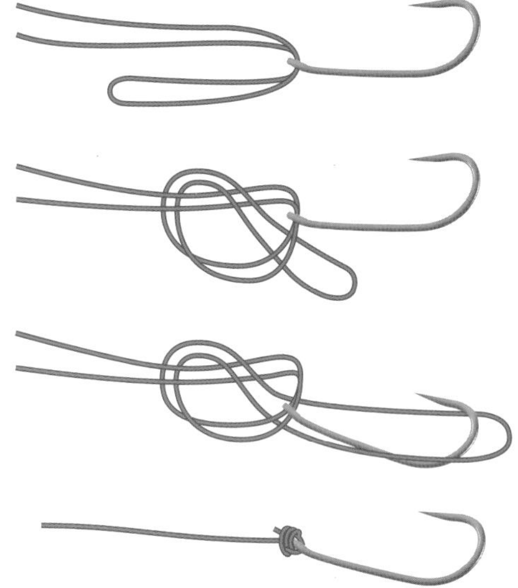

PARSONS, ROY

Fishery manager at the popular Linear Fisheries, Roy is a friend to all of us at Total Carp and Advanced Carp Fishing magazines. He's a great bloke who points literally thousands of carp anglers every year in the right direction when fishing the venue. Whether or not they take any notice is often another matter, but Roy will always try and put you on to fish!

PARTICLES

Seed, pulse and nut baits used in carp fishing. These can either be purchased in their dry form and prepared for fishing, or more often these days they are bought ready-prepared from one of the bigger bait companies.

Tiger nuts, hemp, corn, maize, groats, brazils, tares and even mixtures of multiple particles are just some of the more popular examples.

Not for the first time in the encyclopaedia, we would stress that you should always prepare particles properly and thoroughly. There are plenty of websites that include correct particle preparation guides, including *www.ccmoore.com*, the bait and seed supplier referred to elsewhere in this book. If in doubt, don't use it. Besides, it is much more convenient to buy the prepared stuff these days.

PASTE

When carp anglers refer to paste they are usually talking about the mixed paste formed when a base mix and eggs are combined. This paste is then rolled and boiled to form what we all know as boilies.

Many anglers will keep some paste in its pre-rolled-and-boiled form and use it to wrap around their hook baits. This paste breaks down fairly quickly and so increases the attraction around the hook bait itself.

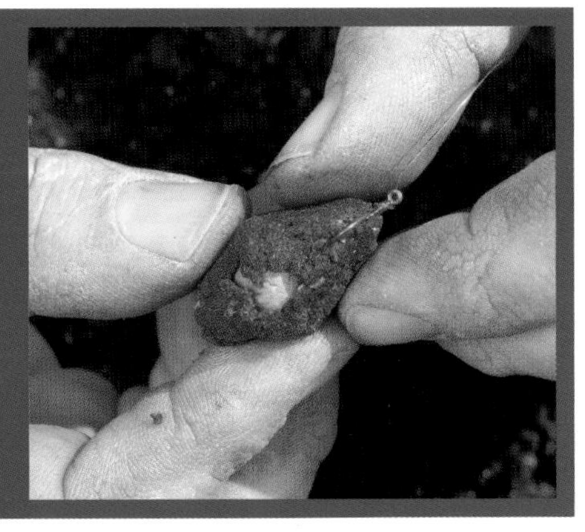

PEANUTS

Popular carp bait for many years, although not used so much these days. Even more than tiger nuts, many waters ban the use of peanuts, not just because of fears over their incorrect preparation, but in the case of the peanut they are said to be carcinogenic. This is one reason why peanuts should never be used in large quantities, although most carp anglers believe that they are most effective when used sparingly anyway.

PELLETS

Most pellets have been adopted from the animal-feed industry, although with the rise in popularity of their use in fishing, many are now specifically designed with angling in mind, especially carp angling.

There are literally hundreds of varieties, from trout and halibut pellets, to coarse pellets, sweetcorn pellets, fruit-flavoured pellets and very often pellets designed to match a particular boilie recipe.

Some are high in oil content, and these should not be used in excess quantities or in winter, whereas others have virtually no oil at all.

Many of the flavoured pellets are extruded prior to the flavours themselves being added, but a few will have the flavours added at the mixing stage. Either way, pellets remain an effective, and often cheap, carp-catching bait.

PEPERAMI

The meat-based snack is a popular bait used by carp anglers. Carp adore it, and it seems to have a particularly good track record in the winter.

PHOTOGRAPHS

The next carp you catch could be the fish of a lifetime, so make sure you get some good snaps. Once the carp is returned these will be the only record of your capture – apart from the obligatory fisherman's tale, of course!

POD

Portable structure used to support rods. While they're specifically designed for firm ground, wooden platforms or gravelly swims where the use of bank sticks is impossible, lots of anglers use their pod whatever the conditions.

Gardner Tackle was one of the first, possibly the very first, inventors of the rod pod, but lots of companies now produce them.

POLARISING SUNGLASSES

Specifically it is the lenses in such glasses that are said to be polarising. This means that they reduce the glare from water's surface area, thus making it easier for the wearer to see through the upper layers and spot fish.

Every carp angler should own a pair of polarising glasses as they make spotting fish and finding marginal spots much easier. In fact, this can be almost impossible without the use of such glasses.

Lots of companies produce polarising sunglasses these days, ranging from high-spec expensive versions down to cheaper ones that, while maybe not quite so effective, can cost less than £10 in some cases.

POP-UPS

The term used to describe buoyant hook baits, which literally 'pop up' to the surface if not weighted down. Used by most anglers in some variety.

PRAM-HOOD BIVVIES

Originally invented by Chris Manifold, this refers to the modern bivvy design that works on a cantilever-style basis similar to the hood of a pram. The poles are laid on the floor, connected together and then pulled forwards in one movement, to form the distinctively shaped design. There are few, if any, bivvy manufacturers who do not now copy this design principle and it is widely regarded as the most complete design on the maket.

PREBAITING

The act of introducing bait over a period, short or long, before a fishing trip. Many of the top anglers lay great store in prebaiting and it's often said that time spent doing this is far more valuable than time spent fishing.

Introducing bait on a regular basis to similar areas helps build the carp's confidence in eating that bait. The more they eat without being caught, the more confident they become and, usually, the easier they become to catch on that bait.

Prebaiting can be either cheap or expensive, but it is also better to put some bait in than none at all.

PRESSURE *(angler)*

This refers to the weight in numbers of carp anglers on a lake at any given time. Lakes that are busy are said to see lots of angler pressure and this can have an effect on the carp in said lakes.

Carp that are regularly fished for by large numbers of anglers can become more difficult to catch. Whether this is through some intelligence or purely by association with danger is a long-standing argument, but either way it tends to remain.

Angler pressure has a huge effect on the behaviour of carp and they will act according to the influence of angler pressure on their natural environment, not least because of the disturbance.

PROLOGIC *(company)*

Manufacturer of a wide range of carp fishing tackle, including rods, bivvies, luggage, terminal tackle and much more. Website: *www.prologicfishing.com*

PRESSURE *(atmospheric)*

Also referred to as air pressure, this refers to the downforce exerted against a surface by the air above it. Literally this translates to anglers as that pressure exerted on the waters that we fish. This air pressure has a direct effect on the water pressure that is, naturally, exerted on the creatures within it.

Air pressure has a huge effect on the behaviour of carp and it is a science in itself to explain. However, in raw layman's terms, periods of low pressure tend to be more productive than high-pressure ones. During high-pressure spells carp will often find their comfort zone in mid-water and tend not to feed so heavily. This is a sweeping generalisation, but it helps to understand why some days are more productive than others.

PVA

PVA stands for Poly Vinyl Alcohol and is used to form threads or sheets of material which melt in water. Although not invented for the angling market, it has been adopted and developed into numerous useful items, the main two being mesh-stocking PVA and solid PVA bags. Also, PVA tape, string and cloth are also used in carp fishing.

Solid PVA bags are filled with bait and often have the baited rig and lead also secured inside. PVA mesh is also filled with bait items, including boilies, and then nicked on to the hook prior to casting. In both cases, once on the lake bed the PVA begins to melt, releasing all of the free offerings in close proximity to the baited rig.

After the hair rig, PVA must surely be one of the most influential introductions to carp fishing in recent years, and is used by thousands of anglers.

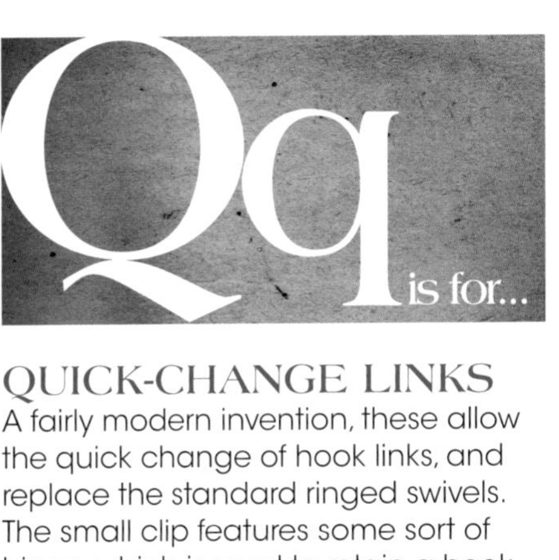

Qq is for...

QUICK-CHANGE LINKS

A fairly modern invention, these allow the quick change of hook links, and replace the standard ringed swivels. The small clip features some sort of hinge, which is used to retain a hook link with a loop tied in the end.

Very many manufacturers produce one version or another of quick-change clips and they are extremely popular with the modern carp angler.

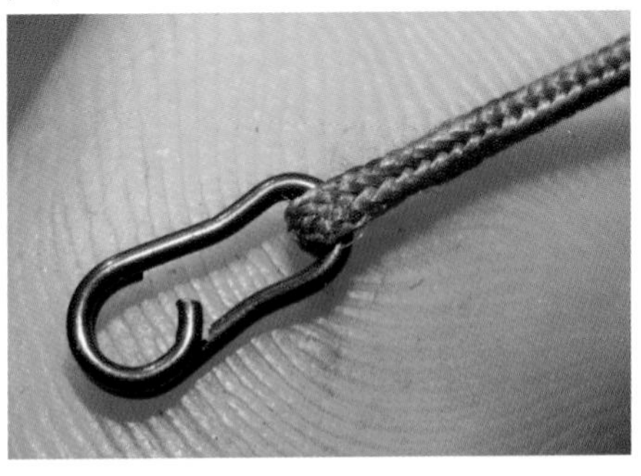
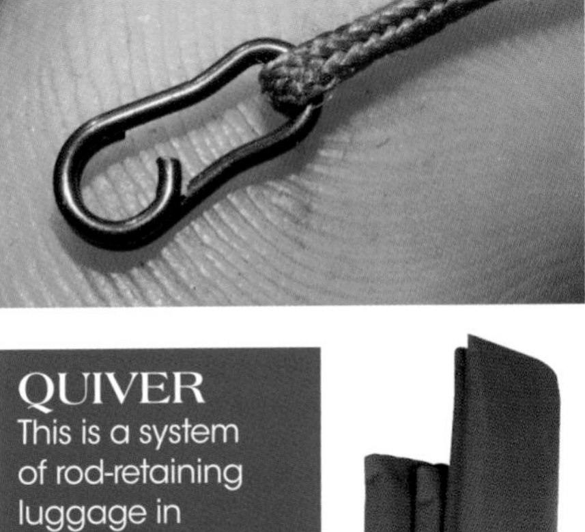

QUIVER

This is a system of rod-retaining luggage in which, instead of housing the rods inside a central compartment, they are held on the outside of the main body, often in removable sleeves. The central compartment is then used to house a bivvy or similar shelter.

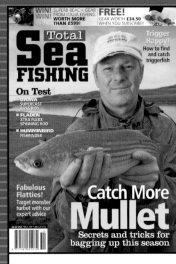

READYMADES

Strictly speaking this refers to any pre-rolled boilies that you can buy from shops, ready to use. However, more commonly it is used to refer to the shelf-life readymades, which do not require freezing as they inherently contain preservatives.

Although the overwhelming majority of carp anglers believe that the frozen versions are more effective and of more appeal to carp, readymades continue to outsell them by at least 10 to one.

This is mostly due to their convenience, as you do not have to freeze them, either before or between trips. This means that the angler can open a bag, take them fishing, and retain any unused baits.

Readymades are generally a little cheaper than freezer baits as well, further adding to their appeal. Finally, there are a much wider number of flavours available in readymade boilies, and many entice the angler to buy them more than they necessarily entice the carp to eat them!

READY-TIED RIGS/LEADERS

Typically of modern society, just about everything you need to use in carp fishing these days is available pre-made. This makes them ultra convenient and removes most of the effort on the part of the angler.

Such products include rigs and leaders, many of which are now available pre-tied from most manufacturers of the individual items. Leaders come complete with lead clips or helicopter rig components in place, and ready-tied rigs are of an extremely high quality these days.

REDMIRE POOL

Hugely famous, Herefordshire carp water that is the Mecca of modern carp angling. Richard Walker, Ritchie Macdonald and Chris Yates are just a few famous anglers who have trodden its paths and recounted the experience in various writings. The Passion For Angling series on terrestrial television also thrust it into a wider limelight.

REED BEDS

There are a few varieties of reed that line the banks of UK stillwaters and rivers, the more common of which includes Norfolk Reed (phragmites) and this can be found on a huge majority of gravel pits.

Carp love to patrol margins and like to use the cover of reeds, and the inherent natural food which lives on them, and will spend hours in reeds. Provided you do so safely, the edges of reed beds are great places to place a baited rig.

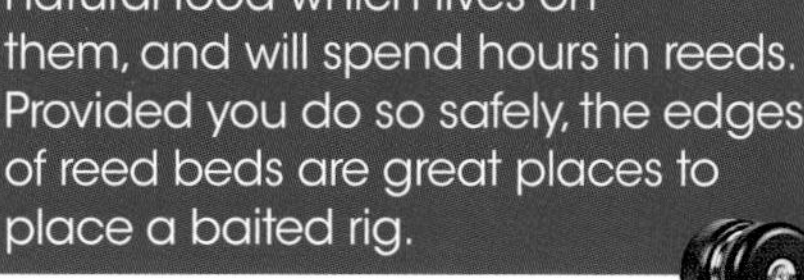

REELS

The earliest record of reels being used comes in a painting by the Chinese artist Ma Yuan back in 1195. In a nutshell, the reel performs the simple task of storing, deploying and retrieving fishing line, but the modern versions do it with aplomb. Free-spool facilities, bale-arm evolution, materials, clutches, bearings and much more continue to add to the near-space-age features on modern reels. There is a wide range of models available to suit various fishing styles and anglers' budgets. The best-known companies producing modern reels are Shimano and Daiwa, but there are dozens of companies that sell reels under their own brand names these days.

REHYDRATED BAITS

Although used for many years, only in the last decade have rehydrated baits been written about in magazines and, so, gained in popularity among the masses.

Essentially, they are boilies that have been dried out and then rehydrated with liquid at a later date. This is done for a few reasons. Firstly, baits are dried out to help preserve them on longer trips, and then rehydrated with flavours or additives, and water, to bring them back to their original state for fishing.

Also, and this can be done on any trip, by adding a variety of liquids the profile of the bait itself can be altered. Finally, and the most written about tactic, is to simply soak the baits in water for up to a day or two in order that they 'wash out' and give the appearance of a bait that has been in the lake for some time. This is thought to fool carp into thinking that the bait is old and so safe to eat, on the presumption that the angler who deposited it there has long since gone home!

Of course, carp do not have the ability to rationalise that argument, but associating fresh new bait with capture can lead them to follow this behaviour. Or are we thinking far too deeply? Well, many top carp anglers put great store in this washed-out baiting principle.

RENYARD, STEVE

Well-known carp angler, perhaps best known for his exploits on the renowned Withy Pool, where he invented the famous Withy rig, specifically intended to target the residents of that venue. The rig is still widely used and slight variations of it can be found in many carp anglers' rig boxes.

RICHWORTH *(company)*

One of the original boilie-producing bait companies and the first to roll and sell baits on an industrial scale. When Richworth first introduced its perfectly round, uniformly rolled and flavoured Tutti Frutti boilies, users dominated waters up and down the country. Thus, the modern boilie phenomenon was born. Website: *www.richworth.com*

Richworth

RIGS

Made up of a hook-link material and hook, the rig is specifically the bit at the very end of the line, which is pre-tied by the angler (unless using a ready-tied version) and which provokes much discussion in the carp fishing world.

There are literally hundreds of rig variations in use, made from a baffling array of materials, and each angler believes his to be the one that catches more than the rest. That does not stop him trying everybody else's at some point, though!

RIG BIN

Item used to store rigs, specifically chod-type rigs. These are usually a tub with some form of central hub that the rigs wrap around, maintaining a curved shape, and secured with a pin or suchlike to an inner foam section. Gardner and Fox each produce excellent rig bins for chod rigs and similar.

RIG RINGS

Small, metal rings that are incorporated into many modern carp rigs. On a D-rig for example, a ring is used on the mono loop attached to the hook and the hook bait is then tied to this using bait floss.

RIG WALLETS

Luggage item used to store the plethora of rigs that modern carp anglers employ. This can include firm boards that stiff rigs are attached to, as well as clear wallets which more supple rigs can be stored in. There are dozens available, in various sizes, and some are even solid-plastic 'boxes', such as the Korda Rig Safe.

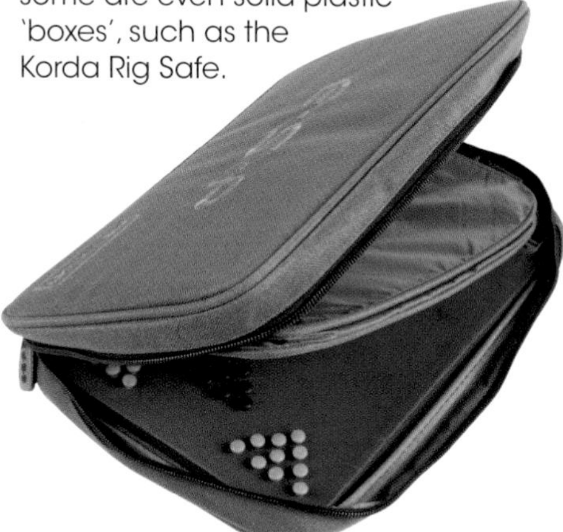

RING SWIVEL

This is a swivel that, at one end, features a larger ring. Ostensibly these are designed to offer the attached rig more freedom of movement, but they are used extremely regularly on a variety of rigs.

RITCHIE, DEREK

Lovable carp angler who has been the star of many carp fishing magazines and films over the last decade or two. Although his larger-than-life personality is the first thing that many people associate with Derek, he is a hugely talented carp angler who has been catching fish for over 50 years. He is also a smashing chap and will go out of his way to help anglers on the bank.

RIVERS/RIVER CARP

Carp are more and more prevalent in the UK's rivers these days and have soon adapted to master that environment. Following the floods of 2007 many carp lakes burst their banks and carp moved freely between them, often coming to finish up in river systems the nation over.

Still rarely targeted by carp anglers, rivers can be a brilliant option in the search for big carp. However, they do require a slightly different approach to stillwater angling, but learning the ways of rivers and then catching their resident fish is an immensely enjoyable pastime.

ROBIN RED
Hugely popular and much documented bait additive, it's actually used in bird foods to develop colour in exotic ornamental species. Slightly spicy, it is widely used in carp baits these days, especially the red ones.

There is much discussion over various versions of robin red, but the original is still widely credited as being specific to Haith's, the seed merchant.

ROD-BOX *(company)*
New company producing car roof boxes specifically shaped to accommodate carp rods. The elongated design is perfect for storing made-up rods in holdalls or suchlike on trips abroad. They're also very handy for sessions closer to home, especially if you have a small car into which you normally have to cram the rods. Website: *www.rod-box.co.uk*

rod-box.co.uk

RODS
Most modern carp rods are constructed from carbon blanks with reel seat, rings and handle attached. Choosing which rod to buy can be a minefield for the modern angler as such things as test curve, action and price all play a huge factor. Ask in your local tackle shop for advice on these. See Test Curve for more details.

ROD LICENCE
Anyone wanting to fish freshwater venues in this country is required to purchase an Environment Agency rod licence. These are bought from most larger Post Office branches or direct from the EA website and, at the time of writing, cost £27 each. One licence covers you to use up to two rods, so if you intend fishing with three rods, as many carp anglers do, then you are required to purchase two licences.

ROLLING COMPANIES
Suppliers of rolled baits on a commercial level. As well as the bait manufacturers themselves, many companies offer bait-rolling services, either with commercial recipes or varieties of their own. Many will roll, for example, a Mainline bait but offer a personalised service whereby they can add a particular ingredient or maybe roll sizes that are not available in the shops. There are some big bait-rolling firms, such as Kent Particles, but the majority work on a more local level.

ROLLING MACHINE

When producing bait in large quantities, such as the big bait companies and larger bait rolling firms, industrial-sized machines are used to roll huge quantities of bait at a time. Often, one run through the machine will produce 30kg of finished baits!

ROLLING TABLE

These are what are used to roll baits in smaller quantities and can be table sized, such as the Shilham versions, or even smaller hand-held models such as the hugely popular Gardner versions.

RUNNING RIGS

Refers to a presentation where the lead runs freely on the line or leader. There are advantages and disadvantages to this system, as there are with all setups.

RULES

Many fisheries will have numerous rules to which any visiting anglers must adhere. These range from guidelines on which areas of water to cast to, right through to rules and bans concerning tackle and bait use. See also: bans.

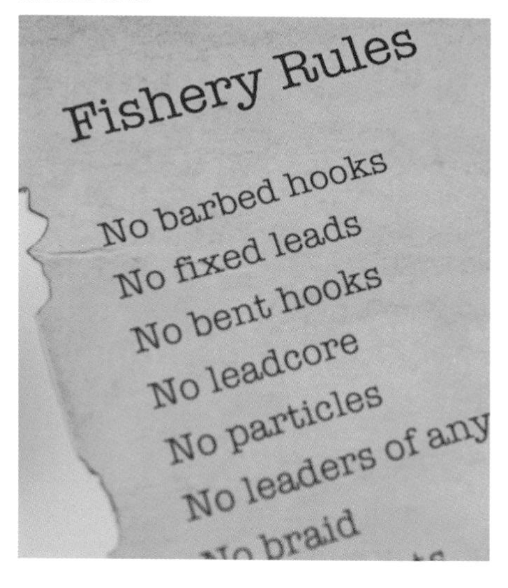

Fishery Rules
No barbed hooks
No fixed leads
No bent hooks
No leadcore
No particles
No leaders of any
No braid

RUSSELL, IAN

Hugely successful and respected carp angler, who fills the regular Troubleshooter slot in Total Carp magazine. He is the twice-former champion of Battlecarp, a tournament in that magazine which pitched many of the top anglers against each other in a knockout format. Nobody ever beat Ian in this series of matches.

The heart-stopping
moment where success
edges closer and closer...

SABER *(company)*

Supplier of carp tackle, predominantly luggage and rods, which are well made but with budget in mind. Website: *www.sabertackle.com*

SALT

It has long been known that carp require an element of salt in their diets, as do any animals, but in recent years much has been made of this in carp literature.

Salt is often added to boilie mixes, spod mixes and groundbaits – in fact, some anglers even use it neat in a PVA bag!

However, there is a big difference between table salt and the natural form of salt as carp find in their everyday diets, and sometimes anglers use salt as much to look like they know what they're doing as much as they do to catch more carp.

At certain times of year carp need extra salt in their diets and, at these times, the addition of proper salt to baits can be a huge edge. Beyond that, however, treat salt no differently to any other bait additive or ingredient.

SATNAV

Love them or loathe them, a satnav can be a massive help when finding your way to a new venue, especially if it's in the back of beyond!

SECRET SQUIRRELS

The term 'secret squirrel' is used to describe an angler who not only keeps himself to himself, but also keeps his tactics and catch rate secret. They tell nobody about their captures and offer no help or guidance to other anglers on the water.

SELF-TAKE PHOTOGRAPHY

The more you go fishing on your own, the more important it is to learn how to take your own pictures. Many cameras have self-take facilities, either on a timer or sometimes via a small remote-control unit.

It's well worth investing in such a camera and then in some time to get used to using it. Otherwise, if you catch the carp of a lifetime and there is nobody around to take the snaps for you, the chance to record the feat will pass.

SCALES *(fish)*

Most fish are covered in scales, a protective outer plating that forms part of the exterior skin. Scales vary in size from one fish to another. Common carp are covered in them, mirrors have some and leather carp have none.

Scales offer protection from disease, temperature changes and other external influences. It is said that because they have no scales, leather carp are more prone to the cold and so they will continue to eat more in order to maintain their metabolic status quo. This can lead them to being easier to catch in colder conditions.

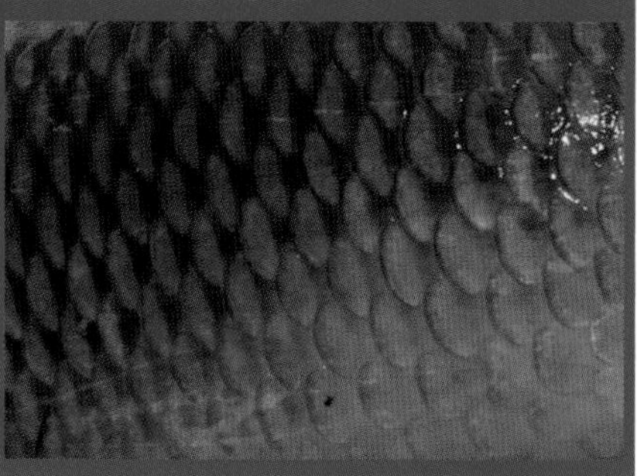

SCALES *(weighing)*

Device used to weigh carp. As well as the traditional dial and spring scales, these days there are several digital versions available.

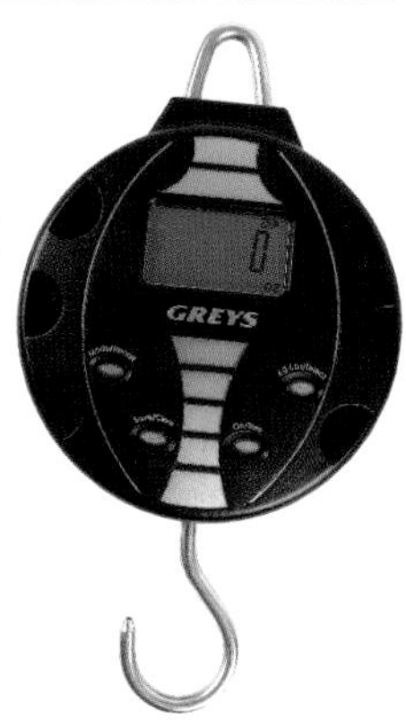

SHELF-LIFE BAITS

These are boilies that have preservatives inherent in their ingredients, and so last a lot longer than frozen baits.

Although most carp anglers agree that freezer baits are more effective and better for the carp nutritionally, shelf-life baits still sell in far higher numbers due to their convenience and the fact that you can re-use them once opened. See also: Readymades.

SHELLEY, JIM

One of the most successful carp anglers of his generation, Jim has been responsible for the capture of huge numbers of carp, large and small. He runs tuition days that are proving extremely popular, not least because his pupils invariably catch something, and often something big!

SILT

In a nutshell, this is soil-like material on the lake bed and is formed by deposits of natural material over long periods of time. The fresher the silt, the more likely it is to contain numbers of natural fauna, much of which the carp will feed on. Old, stagnant silt, however, is of little interest to carp.

Silt can be extremely deep on some venues, particularly older venues surrounded by trees, and specific rigs are designed to effectively present baits in such deep silt.

Other, newer lakes will still have plenty of areas of silt, especially between bars and plateaus on gravel pits, and these are definitely worth exploring as areas to present your baits.

SHIMANO *(company)*

SHIMANO

Manufacturer of a huge range of fishing tackle, but most notably its market-leading reels. Shimano is synonymous with reels and many, many carp anglers use their big-pit versions for carp fishing. As well as reels, Shimano produces clothing, rods, luggage and line. Website: *www.shimano-eu.com*

SINGLES

No, it's not a dating agency for carp anglers, singles is short for single hook baits. These are literally a hook bait that is used with no free offerings and is often cast at showing fish. While the most commonly used are high-attract versions, a normal boilie can be just as effective, especially if dipped or soaked before use.

SIZE

Whether or not the size of fish is important is down to the individual angler. However, many lay huge importance on the size and weight of the carp that they catch and tend to weigh most of their captures in order to 'give them a number'.

SLACK LINES

As it suggests, this refers to the style of fishing where the main line is left slack while the baits are out. Once you've cast out the rig, dip the rod tip under the water and allow the line to start sinking. You'll need to pay a little line off so that this happens effectively. Don't rush things and be sure that all of the line has sunk to the bottom before even considering attaching your bobbin to the line.

The main reason why most employ the tactic, is to keep the line out of harm's way with everything pinned to the lake bed so as not to spook carp. Also, in some situations, especially with mono, it can be more sensitive in terms of bite detection when a carp picks up the rig and moves away from the angler. However, drop-back bite indication can actually be adversely affected when slack lining.

Snapshot of slack lines

1 Once you have cast out your rig, take some time to allow the line to sink fully.

2 Once all of the line has sunk, place the rod on the alarm and clip on your bobbin.

3 Let some line off, allow it to settle, then let some more off until everything is slack...

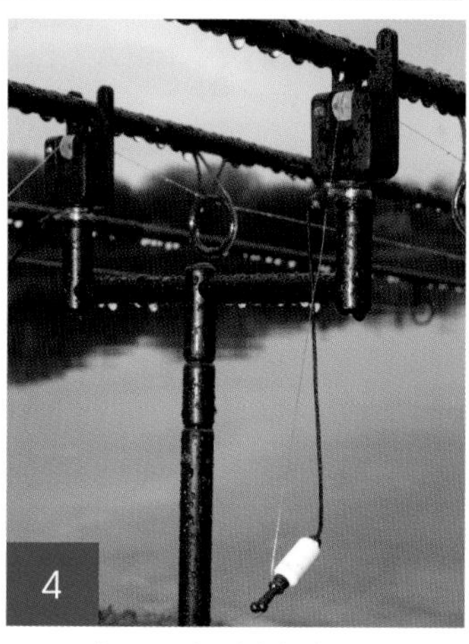

4 ... and your bobbin hangs completely limp, like this. There, you're now slack lining!

SMITH, NEIL

Northwest-based carp angler and a regular in the Northern Monkeys feature slot in Total Carp magazine. Neil is rated highly as a carp angler and it has often been said that were he to live in the southeast, with the abundance of big carp available to him, he would be one of the biggest names in carp fishing.

Neil used to own a bait-rolling company and knows more than a thing or two about bait, its application and how to catch carp on it. He's also a gifted angler of other species.

SNAGS

This refers to root systems, fallen trees and other obstacles which carp use for cover. If fishing near to snags always do so responsibly and with the right gear.

SOAKS

Liquid attractants that baits are left in for long periods to increase their attraction or to alter their profile. It's this long-term use that differentiates a soak from a dip or glug.

SOCIAL NETWORK SITES

Thousands of carp anglers keep in touch via Facebook and suchlike and the platform is fast replacing traditional web forums. If you're not on Facebook then you might be missing out on the latest chat from carp anglers in your area and beyond.

facebook.

SOCIALS

This refers to gatherings in a particular angler's swim and can range from serene chats over a cup of tea to full-blown, on-the-bank partying. Whatever the case, be sure to always fish safely, act responsibly and do not disturb other anglers on the venue.

SOLAR TACKLE *(company)*

Martin Locke's Kent-based company is responsible for tackle and bait items, but is perhaps best known for its range of stainless-steel rod-support products, bite indicators and some very successful baits, such as Club Mix and Winter Secret.
Website: *www.solartackle.co.uk*

SONUBAITS *(company)*

Relatively new bait company that is already making a name for itself with groundbait, pellets and liquid carp catchers. Website: *www.sonubaits.com*

SPAWNING

The age-old ritual of mating. When fish are spawning they have little else on their mind and you can kiss goodbye to tempting them into snaffling your carefully prepared baits. In fact, if the carp are spawning then anglers should leave them to it, unmolested. Many waters close to anglers during periods of spawning and immediately afterwards. It can be a pretty stressful affair for the fish and they need time to recover.

SPODDING

Although utilised by carp anglers for some time before, spodding really came of age in the 2000s and now it seems that every carp angler owns and uses a spod. The spod itself is a rocket-shaped receptacle that attaches to the end of the line and is cast out, full of bait. It flies through the air, lands and then the buoyant nose forces it to sit upright in the water, thus emptying its load.

Masters of the tactic can deposit large quantities of bait on tight spots at significant ranges, but spodding can also be effective at shorter distances. Lots of different spod sizes and designs are available currently.

SPRINGATE, PETE
Pioneering carp angler of the 1960s to 1980s and captor of very many of the nation's most famous carp from waters such as Yateley, Wraysbury, Yeoveney, Harefield and many more. Pete, often referred to as 'Sir Pete', is one of the most highly respected carp anglers of all time.

STICKS (PVA)
Some debate exists over who 'invented' the tactic but it was certainly championed in its early years by Nick Helleur. Shortly after the introduction of mesh-type PVA, specifically the narrower 'boilie' version, groundbait was mixed to a suitable consistency and used to fill a short section of the PVA itself, which was then tied off tightly at each end and the rig threaded through it to increase attraction and help avoid tangles.

Due to its appearance, as well as the fact that Nick was then sponsored by Dynamite Baits, the resulting parcel was christened the Dynamite Stick. This has subsequently been shortened to just 'stick'. Sticks can be just an inch or so in length or indeed can be used as long as you wish, and they are generally threaded on to the hook link prior to casting.

STICKY *(company)*
Bait manufacturer perhaps best known for its bloodworm ranges of boilies, pellets, groundbaits and liquids. Sticky also makes successful baits such as Vor-Tex and XS. Website: *www.stickybaits.com*

STALKING
Ultra short-range carp fishing tactic, often involving the targeting of fish just inches or feet from the bank.

Stealth tactics are required for this often heart-stopping tactic. There are few more exciting ways of catching carp than when you can single them out and even watch them pick up your baited rig.

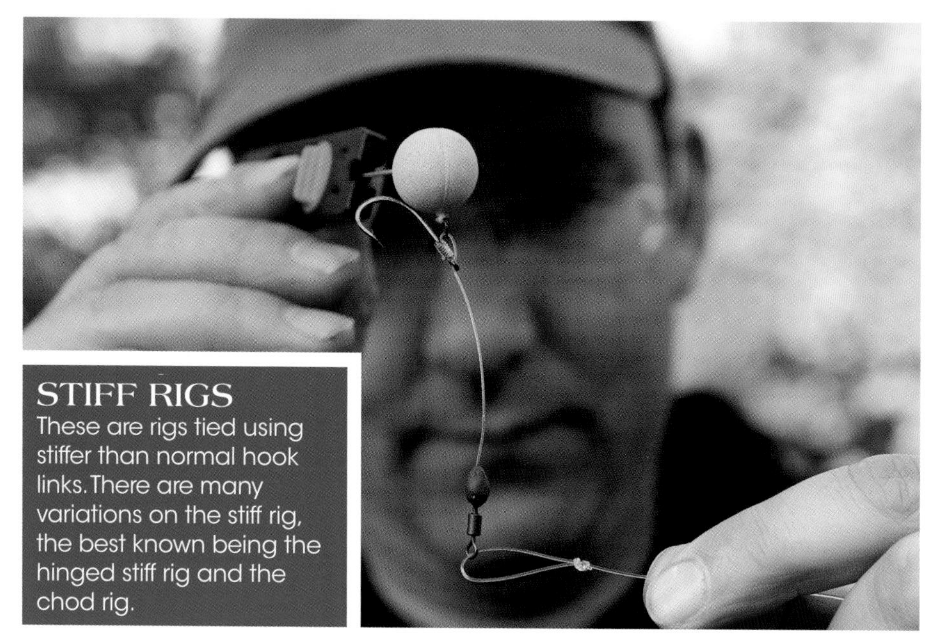

STIFF RIGS
These are rigs tied using stiffer than normal hook links. There are many variations on the stiff rig, the best known being the hinged stiff rig and the chod rig.

STORM POLES
Extended banksticks that are used to support brollies and some bivvy systems. They attach to the front of the shelter and then stick into the ground, offering increased rigidity and strength.

STOVE

Small cookers used to cook food, boil a kettle and perhaps to keep warm in the depths of winter. Both gas-burning and fuel-burning stoves are available, the latter of which can be used with simple unleaded petrol or dedicated burner fuel.

The gas versions either screw into the top of a gas can or attach via a short hose. These run off butane/propane mixtures that are efficient burners, but which can be less effective in particularly cold conditions.

There are many stoves available from tackle companies, outdoor shops and even supermarkets, and some have more than one burner!

STRINGERS

This refers to the use of PVA string with boilies threaded on to it and cast out into the lake. For many years stringers were a hugely popular, and effective, tactic, but more recently the advent of the stick and solid bags has led to their use being dramatically reduced. However, a stringer can still be a brilliant tactic and the fact that fewer anglers use them is all the more reason for you to do so.

Stringers can involve two or more baits, as many as you choose in fact, but it's worth noting that more than three to five can be a bit of a nightmare to cast out, particularly if you are looking for accuracy at longer ranges.

SUFIX *(company)*

Huge multinational company that is a market leader in the manufacturer of fishing lines, including braids and monofilaments. Website: *www.sufix.com*

SURFACE FISHING

The targeting of fish on the lake surface, using buoyant baits such as pop-ups, dog biscuits and floating pellets, along with specialised floater kit.

SWEETCORN

Undoubtedly one of the very best carp baits of all time, with the bonus of being nice to eat should you feel that way inclined!

Its bright yellow appearance, sweet taste and soft texture make it almost irresistible. Combined with pellets inside a PVA bag, scattered into the margins or even spodded in quantity, sweetcorn is hugely effective and easy to use. Don't go fishing without at least a can or two of sweetcorn in your bag.

SWEETENERS

Additive ingredients that enhance the sweetness of a bait. Carp are often said to have a fondness for sweet baits, but sweeteners can also work brilliantly to soften the profile of baits with synthetic flavourings as their main component. Examples include Hinders' Betalin, Solar's Candy Cream Sweetener and Mainline's Sweet Ade.

SWIM

Just as match anglers have 'pegs', carp anglers refer to the areas which they fish from as swims. Most lakes will have designated swims dotted around the venue and it's generally expected that you fish from these areas only. Some waters, particularly club or syndicate lakes, will allow you to fish from in between swims, especially when stalking for example, or may have no swims marked out at all, so you can fish where you like.

While day-ticket venues will normally just number their swims, many club and syndicates will give theirs descriptive names, such as Back Bay, The Beeches or The Grassy Double, for example.

SWINGERS

No, this does not refer to groups of carp anglers and their wives chucking car keys into a bait bucket and taking a lucky dip! Instead, it is a term used to describe various bite indicators or 'bobbins'.

SWIVELS

Two rings either side of a rotating body form a swivel. Swivels sit between the main line and the hook link and their primary use is to eliminate line twist. Beyond that, many rigs incorporate swivels to allow more freedom of movement and even a pivot in the rig itself.

There are several varieties of swivel available these days, some with a small and a large rig, many with rings of equal size and some with multiple rings, each of which have a different intended application.

SYNDICATES

These are carp waters that a limited number of fee-paying members have access to. Some syndicates are run by a small group of friends for their own benefit, whereas others are more commercial concerns.

TACKLE

Simply refers to all of the various items that carp anglers use, including rods, reels, hooks, line and pretty much everything else bar the bait.

TACKLE BOX

Most carp anglers carry a tackle box of some description, used to store smaller items of tackle, and ranging from tool boxes bought from the local DIY outlet through to purpose-built, multi-compartment boxes with spaces for all the modern carp angler's essential items.

TAIL

The main fin of the carp, positioned at the rear and which gives the carp its propulsion. Some carp's tails can be enormous, easily bigger than the hand span of even the biggest bloke.

TAKEAWAYS

If you're not one for cooking on the bank then be sure to get the number of the local takeaway. Oh, and find out if they deliver... !

TARGET FISH

This refers to a specific carp that an angler sets out to catch, and doesn't always necessarily have to be the biggest in the lake, but normally it is. Many of the big-name carp anglers fish in this fashion, singling out individual carp in lakes up and down the country and setting off to catch them. This is what leads to so many of the best-known carp anglers having caught the same carp, as the same big carp appear on most of their wish lists.

TEA

Essential sustenance of the carp angler – never go fishing without your tea kit. It's a good idea to take a spare cup or two along with you as well, just in case yours becomes the social swim.

TEFLON COATING

In recent years many hook manufacturers have added a Teflon coating to their hooks. This serves the purpose of dulling the hook itself, so making it less conspicuous or prone to glistening in any sunlight. It also allows the smoother movement of the hook when pricking a carp. The majority of hooks are Teflon coated these days and some companies are even using different coloured versions.

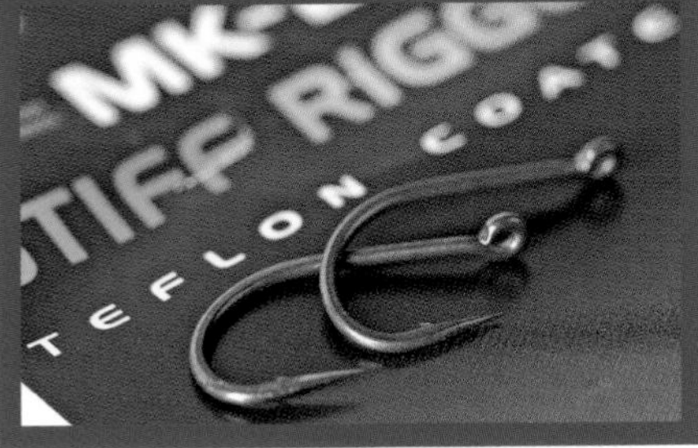

TEMPERATURE

Just one of the climate-related elements that affects the behaviour of carp. This happens in terms of air and water temperature, with the latter often being dictated by the former, and certainly having the biggest effect on the carp themselves.

There has been much written about the effects of temperature on the carp and their environment, too much to try and detail in this listing. However, it's not as simple as carp preferring warm water to cold water.

That said, sustained spells of warmer weather will usually lead to better catch rates than sustained periods of cold, naturally. It's a bit of a minefield!

°C
+70
–40

TENCH

Although any species other than carp are often referred to as 'nuisance' fish, you cannot help but admire the wonderful tench, or 'tinca'. Tench often grow to big sixes these days, into mid-doubles in fact, helped no doubt by the mass introduction of carp baits on a regular basis. Female fish tend to grow larger than the males, but each, with their deep-green flanks, tiny, immaculate scales and telltale blood-red eyes is a sight to behold.

Legend has it that the slime from a tench works to heal wounds on other species, hence their other nickname, the doctor fish.

TERMINAL TACKLE

This refers to the array of smaller tackle items, usually rig bits and pieces, which are used by carp anglers. The sheer range of terminal tackle available to the modern carp angler is mind-blowing and, no doubt, causes much confusion when anglers attempt to decide what to use and what not.

TERRAPIN

Somehow, and there are a few reasons for this, terrapins have been introduced into some waters and, where present, can be a real nuisance. Depending on the species, some can grow to quite significant proportions, and they pack a nasty bite if you put your fingers too close, so beware when unhooking it if you are unfortunate enough to catch one.

TEST CURVE

A fishing rod's test curve is the amount of weight required at the tip to bend the rod through 90 degrees. So, a carp rod with a 3lb test curve would require a weight of 3lb to pull it round.

The higher the test curve the stiffer the blank and, usually, the further it will cast a lead weight. A lot still hinges on the angler's ability, however, as well as the balance of the equipment but this is a good way to differentiate the different test curves on the market.

It's important to balance your lead choice with the test curve of the rod and, again simplistically, you should look to match the test curve in pounds to the weight of the lead in ounces, give or take half an ounce. So, for example, a 3lb test-curve rod is matched with a lead weighing 3 to 3.5oz and so on.

THERMOCLINE

Water temperature is not constant through any given lake and can vary markedly in different areas and, crucially, at different depths. The layers of different temperature water play a significant role in fish behaviour.

At the risk of oversimplifying things, imagine that the middle layer of water is warmer than that at the lake bed or on the surface. Carp can often be found at this particular depth, which could be several feet up or down, and a degree or two warmer than the layers above or below.

A thermocline is a layer of water that markedly differs in temperature from the water above or below it and it is normally used to describe this in the sea or significantly deeper water than most lakes. However, thermocline has become a generic term used by anglers to describe the layered temperature bands that undoubtedly do exist in our lakes.

THERMOMETER

Of course, you know what a thermometer is and what it is used for, but did you know that you can get versions that can be dropped into lakes to test the temperature of the water. Normally on some sort of cord for later retrieval, these can be very handy on occasion. There are even some versions that can be tied to an angler's line and cast out into the lake before being retrieved, complete with reading.

30 PLUS *(company)*

We don't have a chapter with numbers, so we put 30 Plus in here with the T-words. 30 Plus supplies a wide range of carp fishing equipment, often at very affordable prices, including rods, clothing, luggage, terminal tackle and chairs.

Website: *www.specimen30plus.com*

THROWING STICK

A must-have item for the carp angler, a throwing stick is used to feed boilies at ranges up to 100 yards or so. Some really accomplished 'stickers' can get baits out well beyond this, but for the average angler 100 yards is more realistic.

Like an elongated tube (some feature bends in them) the throwing stick works by having boilies dropped inside before thrusting the stick forwards with a sharp movement of the arm. The boilie then fires out of the end of the tube at huge velocity, towards the intended target area. Or at least that's the theory! Throwing sticks can be tricky to master at first, but once you've learnt how to use one they become a vital tool in the bag.

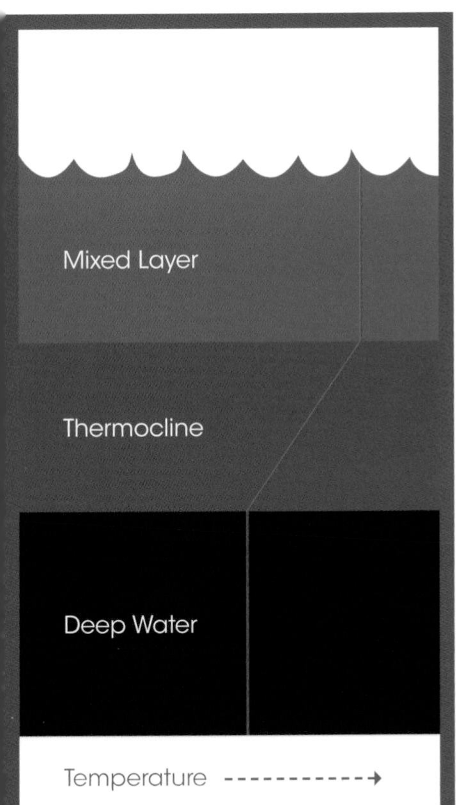

TIGER NUTS

One of the most popular, and effective, particle baits used by carp anglers. Tiger nuts, or 'growlers', are almost irresistible to some carp but, as with any particle bait, you must always make sure that they are properly prepared. These days, it's much easier to buy a large tub of ready-prepared tigers, split them up into smaller bags and freeze them until you need them. To a man, modern carp anglers will tell you that tigers work best in small quantities so don't overdo it when using them.

TIGHT LINES

In contrast to slack lines, tight lines are literally that, and involve the angler fishing with their clutches locked down and the main line tight from the reel to the baited rig.

The debate rages on as to which method, tight or slack, is more successful, when, in fact, they can each be the right tactic on certain days.

TIME BANDITS

Often-derogatory term for near-full-time anglers or those who spend so much time on the bank that they are joked to be 'boring' the carp into submission. In carp fishing, time can be a substitute for skill and the longer you are there the more chance you might think you have of success.

TRAKKER *(company)*

Manufacturer of top-quality bivvies, for which it is best known, as well as luggage, bedchairs, sleeping bags, clothing and other items. Website: *www.trakkerproducts.co.uk*

TORCH

If you are going night fishing then make sure you own one. Simples!

TRAVEL ROD

Either telescopic or multi-piece, these rods break down to a short enough parcel to fit in a suitcase or the boot of a small car.

Although their intended use is when travelling, they're also great to just keep in the car boot on the off chance that a fishing opportunity arises. Lots of manufacturers produce these and they remain extremely popular.

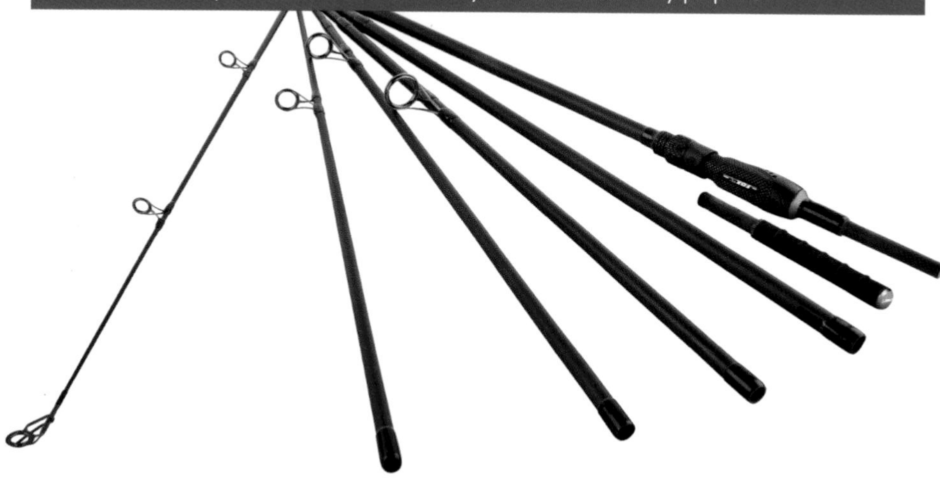

TOTAL CARP

The UK's biggest-selling carp fishing magazine and the place to find all of the latest tackle, tips and tactics to help you catch more and bigger carp. On sale the last Friday of each month, you can subscribe by calling 0845 345 0253 and claim either a discount or a brilliant tackle or bait gift.

TROUBLESHOOTER

Regular feature in Total Carp that has been running for around 10 years and which involves a big-name angler taking novices out and helping them improve their technique and, so, catch more carp.

For the first eight years the job fell to Derek Ritchie and he helped hundreds of anglers catch more, as well as enjoy their fishing. More recently, Ian Russell has taken on the mantle and continues the tradition of passing on key skills to those who accompany him, and all in front of the TC cameras.

TUBING

The two main types of tubing used are either tiny pieces that are used in rig construction or, more commonly in fact, those which the main line is threaded through and which sit just above the lead setup.

This is used for three purposes. Firstly, to stop rigs tangling on the main line during the cast and descent into the water and, secondly, to protect the flanks of carp when they're being played to the bank. Finally, and importantly to the modern carp angler, tungsten-impregnated versions help keep the line pinned hard to the lake bed, out of sight and away from fins and tails.

TWO TONE

At the time of writing, Two Tone, which resided in Mid-Kent Fisheries' Conningbrook, holds the British carp record at 67lb 8oz. Many well-known anglers have cradled Two Tone at some stage and it was on the list of targets for many more before its demise.

Terry Hearn, Lee Jackson, Dave Lane and Jim Shelley all put a number on her in their time, and Lee in fact wrote the wonderful book Just For The Record all about his pursuit of this, the biggest of character fish.

TUNGSTEN PUTTY

Malleable putty that can be added to rigs to help balance hook baits. Kryston was one of the first companies to utilise this putty in a carp fishing sense, but many firms now produce their own versions.

The wax content of the putty dictates how soft and pliable it is, but too much wax can affect buoyancy and adherence, so the balance is essential.

Each manufacturer will claim that theirs is best, but many of them perform the task in hand. As with so many modern tackle items, you will normally find one that you prefer over time and then stick with it.

TUTTI FRUTTI

Although several bait companies, in fact most bait companies, produce a version of tutti frutti in their ranges, the original is a Richworth product.

That Tutti Frutti was the first commercially rolled bait that was given out to 'field testers', who soon dominated waters where it was being used in the south of England. Even to this day, decades on, it remains a potent carp catcher, especially in colder conditions. An absolute classic and a bait that you should try at least once.

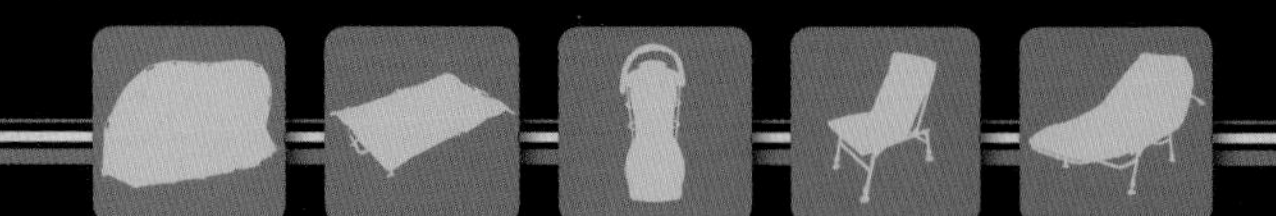

VISION KASHKYM PRO DOME

The design brief was to make "the best 2-man long-stay bivvy on the market." Well here it is – the Kashkym series 2-Man Pro Dome. Featuring 3 'easy-rib' style ultra-light 6061 aerospace-grade aluminium pole supports and tension beams, fully taped seams throughout, reinforced pegging points and new WINDtex fabric technology. The dome has a rubberised heavy-gauge groundsheet where the main body of the bivvy sits. The second groundsheet then clips on, and the integrated twin skin is clipped to the main outer skin forming a formidable and state-of-the-art bivvy system. Featuring heavy-duty T-Bar pegs, a clear infill door panel and a durable carry case.

1-Man Size: 300(W) x 255(D) x 144(H)
2-Man Size: 320(W) x 293(D) x 157(H)

1-MAN £199.99 CODE: UL2242
2-MAN £249.99 CODE: UL1502

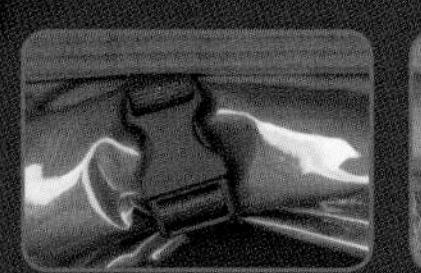

VISION KASHKYM XT TWIN SKIN DOME

The 'Kashkym Series XT' domes from Vision are designed to go up quickly, stay up, and offer maximum protection. Made from super-tough 10,000mm hydrostatic head and 210D Oxford nylon, the twin-skin bivvy features an aerospace-grade aluminium 'easy rib' frame, and a clear and well-thought-out front-door system, allowing easy access. The fully taped seams and triple-stitched pegging points will ensure years of service. The generous carry bag ensures that the bivvy can be packed away with no fuss. Also featuring tensioning bars for added structural rigidity.

1-Man Size: 260(W) x 240(D) x 135(H)
2-Man Size: 300(W) x 250(D) x 145 (H)

1-MAN £139.99 CODE: UL1577 **2-MAN £169.99** CODE: UL1578

KFORE 3-MAN BIVVY

A massive 395cm in width by a depth of 330cm and a height of 175cm, this bivvy is ready for a trip on the Continent. Manufactured using the legendary Windtex material, which is windproof, waterproof and breathable, there is no need to buy an extra winter skin. Supplied with 19mm aluminium poles and PU-coated mozzie net panels, this bivvy offers extremely good value for money, high quality and everything you need from a bivvy for fishing in the UK and foreign climates. Supplied in a heavy-duty carry case.

£229.99 CODE: UL2295

VISION KENWICK ULTRA-LITE 6-LEG BEDCHAIR

The Ultra-Lite 6-leg bed from the Kenwick series focuses on performance. An incredibly lightweight alloy frame, bungee-sprung mattress, swivel mudfeet, multi-point recliner system and extra-padded pillow system makes for a high-quality and high-performance bed.

INCLUDES BODYLINE COMFORT TECHNOLOGY

Size: 80cm wide x 190cm long
Weight: 7kg **Rated to:** 25 stone

£89.99 CODE: UL1501N

VISION KENWICK 6-LEG BEDCHAIR

The 'Kenwick' heavy-duty bed offers a fully adjustable lightweight frame, multi-point recliner system, swivel mudfeet, high-density foam-filled sprung mattress, fully adjustable legs and welly wipe.

INCLUDES BODYLINE COMFORT TECHNOLOGY

Size: 80cm wide x 210cm long
Weight: 9.5kg **Rated to:** 20 stone

£59.99 CODE: UL1200N

A breakthrough in comfort technology. Bodyline offers a double thick layer of built-in FPF foam, strategically postioned to offer high levels of support and comfort to the bodies' stress points.

BEDCHAIRS & CHAIRS STARTING AT ONLY £27.99

VISION KASHKYM BODYLINE XL COMFORT CHAIR

The 'Kashkym' XL Comfort chair offers the ultimate in bankside leisure. The extra-thick padding, arm supports, reclining back and 20cm adjustable legs allow for custom comfort during the longest of sessions, while the extra height in the legs allows for ease of getting in and out of the seating position.

Size: 58cm wide x 75cm overall height (unextended and upright)
Seat height: 45cm
Weight: 7kg
Rated to: 25 stone

£64.99 CODE: UL2199N

INCLUDES BODYLINE COMFORT TECHNOLOGY

VISION KENWICK BODYLINE RECLINER CHAIR

The 'Kenwick' series recliner chair offers a high-density foam-padded base, heavy-duty fabrics, a lightweight frame design, adjustable legs with swivel mudfeet, and a multi-point recliner system to help achieve the perfect sitting angle.

Size: 52cm wide x 75cm overall height (unextended and upright)
Seat height: 30cm
Weight: 4.5kg
Rated to: 20 stone

£39.99 CODE: UL1509N

INCLUDES BODYLINE COMFORT TECHNOLOGY

VISION KENWICK BODYLINE LOUNGER CHAIR

One of the flagship chairs in the 'Kenwick' series, the extra height and width in the chair offers unrivalled support and comfort. The fully padded seating area, and bungee-cord-sprung seat, coupled with recliner adjustment, makes the Lounger one of the most comprehensive chairs available at this price point. Featuring lightweight alloy frame and fully adjustable legs with swivel mudfeet.

Size: 60cm wide x 95cm overall height (unextended and upright)
Seat height: 35cm
Weight: 5kg
Rated to: 25 stone

£44.99 CODE: UL1512N

INCLUDES BODYLINE COMFORT TECHNOLOGY

VISION KENWICK BODYLINE ADJUSTABLE CARP CHAIR

The 'Kenwick' series chair from Vision features a high-density foam-filled back support, heavy-duty fabric, lightweight frame design, adjustable legs and swivel mudfeet.

Size: 48cm wide x 75cm overall height (unextended and upright)
Seat height: 30cm **Weight:** 4.5kg
Rated to: 20 stone

£27.99 CODE: UL1201N

INCLUDES BODYLINE COMFORT TECHNOLOGY

VISION KFORE MEMORY FOAM 6-LEG BEDCHAIR

This is the first bedchair to feature a memory-foam-padded mattress. It has the thickest-ever mattress offering the most comfortable night's sleep available to the modern carp angler. Large removable pillow offers extra head and neck support while the double-corded outer mattress with perforated stitched seams enables the bed to move to every contour of your body.

Size: 85cm wide x 190cm long
Weight: 9.5kg **Rated to:** 30+ stone

£149.99 CODE: UL2237

INCLUDES memoryFOAM COMFORT TECHNOLOGY

VISION FORRESTER 6-LEG BEDCHAIR

Manufactured from our double-density mattress, this bed is one of the most comfortable on the market, with an extra-wide and thick, heavy-duty removable mattress. Perimeter padding is offered by our wintex material, which allows the mattress to breathe, reducing compression and keeping its construction for longer. The frame is manufactured from our lightest alloy that features swivel mudfeet and independent leg adjustment.

Size: 90cm wide x 195cm long
Weight: 9.5kg **Rated to:** 30+ stone

£139.99 CODE: UL2245

INCLUDES BODYLINE COMFORT TECHNOLOGY

VISION

Uu is for...

UMBRELLA

The original shelter of the carp angler, these days the Wavelock-type brollies have been superseded by better versions (see also Oval Brolly) and, of course, bivvies.

The disadvantage with a bivvy is that the internal spines take up so much room and affect headroom. Modern shelters and bivvies do not usually have these spines, so the problem has been largely eradicated.

Some anglers, particularly those who only fish very short sessions or want to be able to pack their shelter down and erect it again in a hurry, still use brollies.

1

2

UNDERARM CAST

Exactly how it sounds, this is a cast made with an underarm action rather than an overhead thump. Ideally suited for accurately placing your baited rig at short range, these are ideal when having to accurately put a bait into a hole in any foliage on close-in island margins and suchlike.

UNDERTOW

This is the effect on the movement of subsurface water caused by the wind. In the simplest example, if the wind is pushing from left to right on a lake, then you'd expect the undertow to go in the opposite direction. The water being pushed one way has to go somewhere and it moves down against the buffering margin, and then changes direction as it hits the lake bed. Remember this is a very simplistic way of describing undertow, but gives you an idea. Undertow can vary greatly at different waters, generally depending on the prevailing winds and the topography of the lake bed. Some waters can suffer from significant undertow and anglers have to consider it when fishing, and other waters might suffer very little.

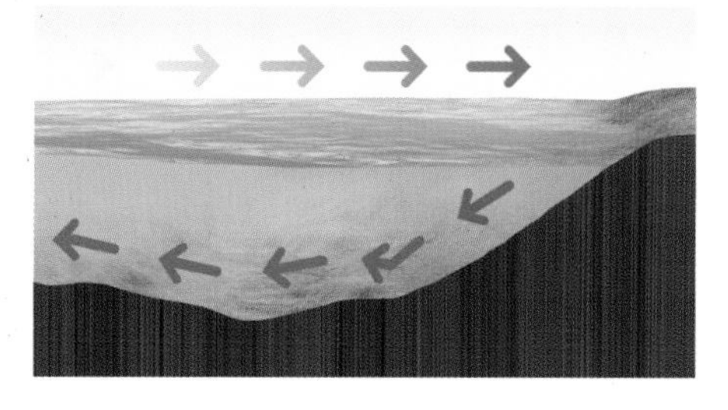

UNHOOKING MAT

An essential item of gear for any carp angler – do not go fishing without one. An unhooking mat should always be used to place the fish on to when unhooking it. You should also take care to hold the fish low down, above the mat, when having photographs taken.

There are very many different types of mat available, with fillings ranging from polystyrene balls (like a bean bag, and thus referred to as beanie mats) to simple foam.

3

VIRGIN WATERS
This refers to waters that have not previously been fished by anglers. A rarity these days.

VENT
A carp's anal passage.

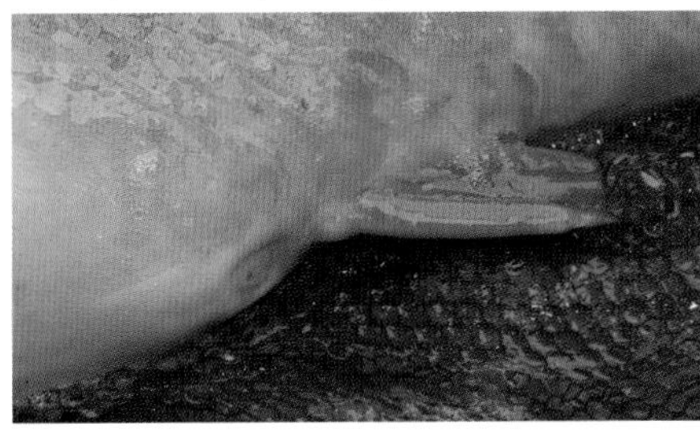

VISION *(company)*
Manufacturer of a wide range of carp fishing equipment, in fact just about everything except rods, reels and terminal tackle at the time of printing. Again, at the time we put this book together, Vision was the principle sponsor of carp catching machine and ACF regular Jim Shelley.
Website: *www.ultimate-direct.co.uk*

VITALIN
This has long been popular with carp anglers and is used as a bulk bait, spod mix and even Method mix. Supplied in huge sacks, Vitalin is actually a dry dog food supplement and includes flaked maize, pellets and several other particles that carp will eat.

It's supplied in its dry form, so should always be soaked before use, but does not normally need the involved preparation that particle baits require.

VORTEX
The pattern, or 'boil' in the water caused by movements of fish, particularly large movements of the fish's tail. Vortexes are obviously a telltale sign of fish activity, but experienced anglers can tell from the nature of a vortex whether it is caused by a feeding fish or a fish that is simply moving through a swim. They can be quite obvious or extremely subtle, so keep your eyes peeled at all times!

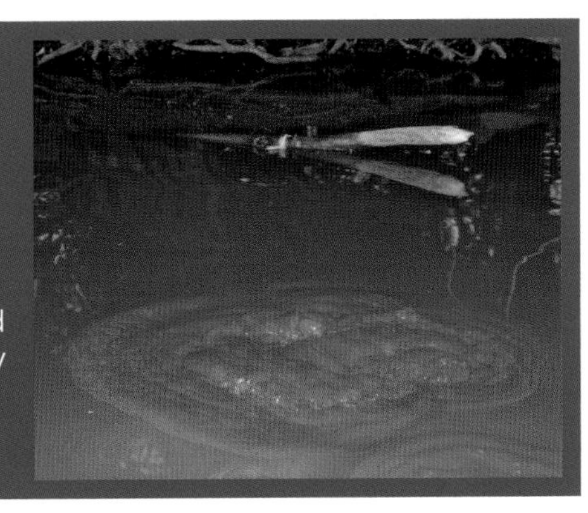

Safely returned to, one day, make
another angler's dreams come true...

Ww is for...

WADERS

Made from rubber, nylon or neoprene, waders are elongated wellies that reach up to knee, waist or even chest high ('chesties'). They are used, unsurprisingly, for wading in the margins, often to place baits but sometimes also to land fish. Always take great care when wading and, if you ever have cause to go out into the lake in a boat, always remove your waders. If you fall overboard while wearing a pair of waders you're in big trouble, as they fill up with water and you'll sink like a stone.

WATER SNAILS

Literally that, snails that live in freshwater. They form a significant part of the carp's natural diet and, when they are present in numbers, can cause the carp to become pre-occupied to the point where they ignore anything else including bait.

WAVERUNNER *(company)*

Popular manufacturer of bait boats, including the Waverunner MK2, Atom and Shuttle.
Website: *www.waverunnerbaitboats.co.uk*

WEBSITES

There are thousands of carp fishing-related websites on the internet, including tackle and bait manufacturers' sites, magazines, forums and much more. Don't forget to check out *www.totalcarpmagazine.com* and *www.advancedcarpfishing.com* for lots of great news, features, advice and competitions!

WALTHAMSTOW

Thames Water-controlled reservoirs in North London and popular day-ticket destinations for carp anglers. 'The ressies' as they are often referred to, are full of big fish, and very many of them are stunners too. At the time of writing, the days-only rule has been lifted for experimental periods and it remains to be seen if this will continue. Whatever the case, Walthamstow is well worth a visit.

WATERCRAFT

This refers to the angler's ability to 'read' the water for signs of fish, both literal and logical. You can only learn watercraft through experience on the bank and, despite trying, no magazine can teach it to you, beyond pointing out some of the most basic elements.

Watercraft is one of the absolute most important aspects of good carp fishing and it is no coincidence that the top carp anglers, such as Dave Lane and Terry Hearn, display watercraft almost beyond compare.

WEATHER

The biggest single influence on carp behaviour. There is no textbook answer to the question of the best weather conditions, as carp remain catchable to some point in all conditions, but tactics often have to be adapted accordingly.

Watch weather forecasts before your trip, and pay particular attention to pressure, wind direction and temperature.

WEED

Evident in some form in most waters, varying from tiny patches to bottom-to-surface forests! There are many different types of weed, but some of the more commonly encountered varieties include Canadian pondweed, silkweed and potamogeton.

Many anglers, particularly the less experienced, are afraid to fish weedy venues, but carp love the stuff and will often feed freely among it. Learn the right tactics and you needn't be afraid of it; in fact, you'll come to view weedy venues with excitement, especially if so many other carp anglers don't visit!

WEIGHING

We all like to put a number on the carp we catch and most anglers will record the weight of any captures. Many then log the rise and fall in a well-known carp's weight, particularly when fishing syndicate venues. Once carp get above 20lb they are seen very much as specimens, but these days 30lb, 40lb and even larger are often the intended quarry.

While it does not necessarily indicate an angler's ability, most people wear their personal best (biggest capture) as a badge of honour. Tragic!

WEIGH SLING

These are used to cradle the carp during weighing. There are hundreds available these days, ranging from some very basic models through to floating versions that can be used for short-term fish retention.

WHEELBARROW

More commonly known as just a barrow (but we missed it out when writing the 'B' section!), anglers use one of these to transport their mountains of gear to and from their swims.

Originally, anglers literally used builder's barrows, but many specialist fishing barrows are now available and they've come quite a way in terms of design over the last decade or so.

WHIPPING KNOT

A type of knot popular with anglers using stiff rigs, in particular the chod rig. It allows a D-rig to be formed without having to pass the line through the hook's eye three times, which can be difficult when using stiff lines.

The whipping knot is notoriously tricky to tie, but once you have mastered it, like most things, it becomes more simple.

Snapshot of the whipping knot

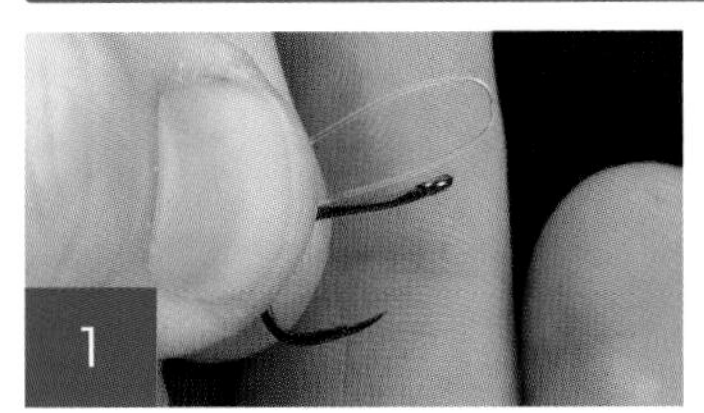

Form a loop in your hook link material along the shank of a hook with an out-turned eye.

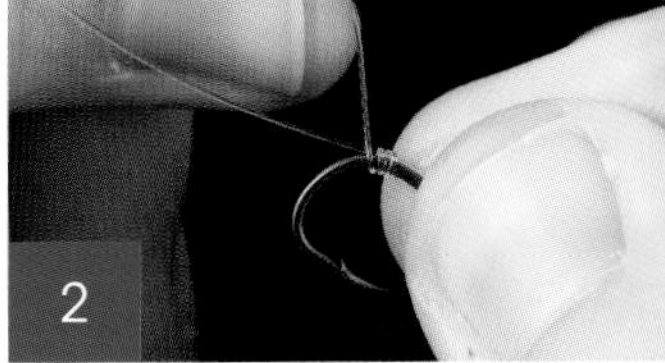

Take one of the tag ends and wrap it around the loop and hook shank five times.

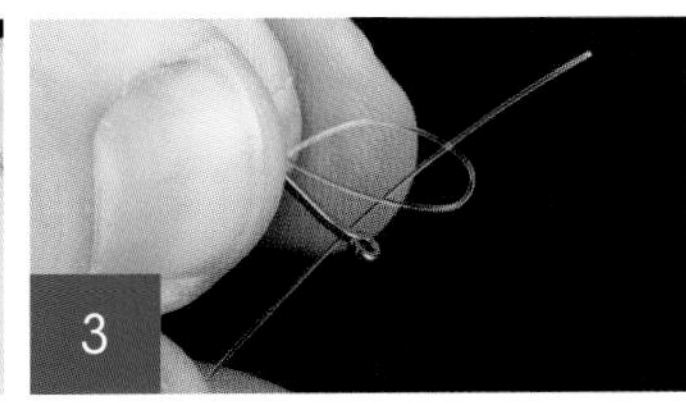

Pass the tag end through the loop formed above the whippings, near the eye.

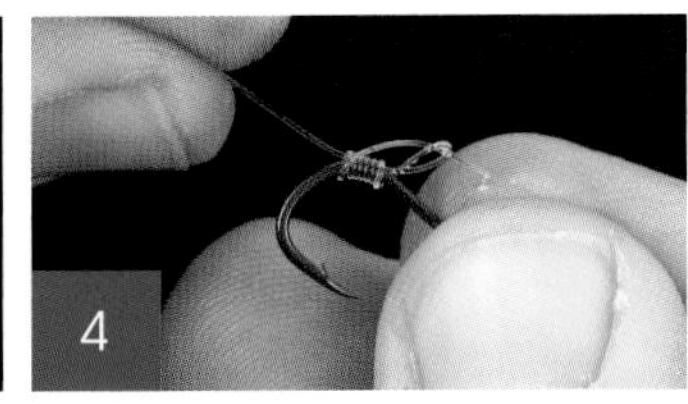

Pull the two tag ends in opposite directions to tighten the knot down...

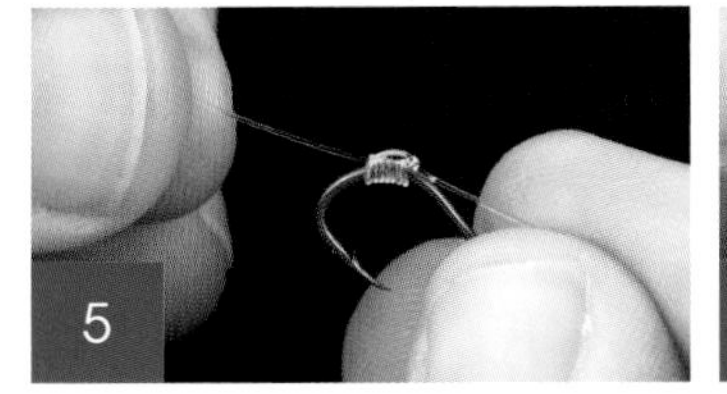

... around the shank of the hook so that it beds down neatly.

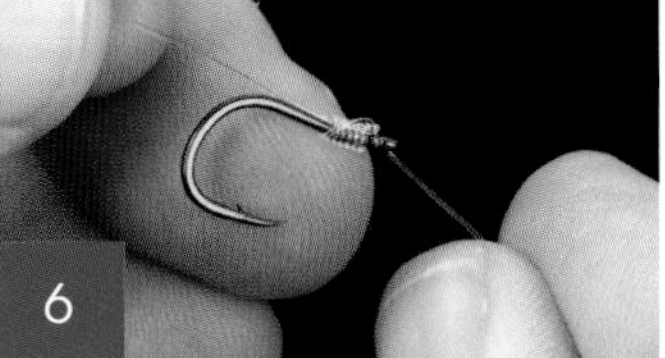

Pass the end of the hook link through the back of the eye and slide the knot down.

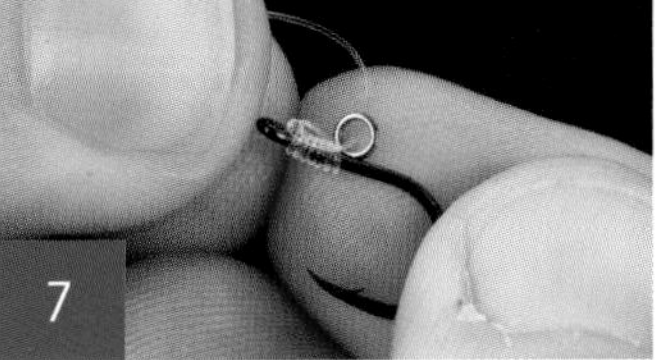

With the knot tight against the eye, pass a rig ring onto the tag end...

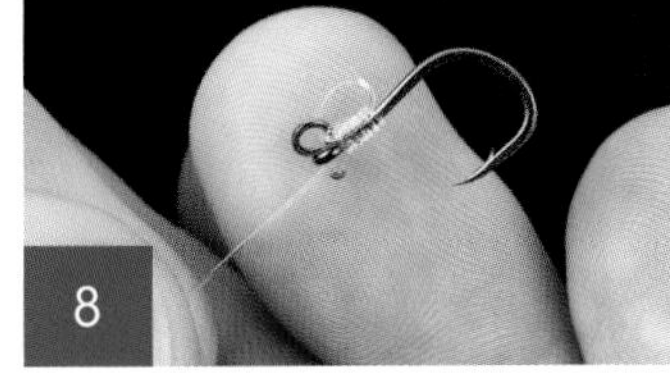

... and then form a D rig with said tag end to complete the rig.

WHIPPINGS

These are the wound filaments that attach the rod's rings (or eyes) to the blank. Usually made from strong cotton or nylon thread, they are usually finished with a varnish or lacquer. Watching a skilled rod builder apply the whippings by hand is fascinating.

WIND

The temperature and direction (the two often go hand in hand) of wind play a significant role in the carp's behaviour. There are some basic guidelines, such as "follow a warm wind" and "fish 'behind' a cold wind", but always be aware that these are exactly that, guidelines. On any given day the carp can equally well throw the textbook out of the window and go completely against your predictions.

WINDWARD BANK

This refers to the bank that a given wind is blowing towards and into. Often the northeast bank is the place to be when a mild southwesterly is blowing, especially if it is a 'new' wind, as the carp will very often follow it in search of food.

WINTER

The time of year when carp fishing can become a bit of endurance test for many. However, on the right venues, carp can still very much be caught in the colder months. Also, with the drop in angler pressure, you will very often have banks or indeed venues to yourself if you venture out.

Choose the right venue, tactics and bait and stay warm and dry, and there is no reason why you cannot enjoy winter carp fishing.

WRAP, PASTE
This refers to a piece of paste being wrapped around the hook bait prior to casting. As the paste – usually the boilie mix prior to having been rolled and boiled – starts to break down it leaks all of its carpy attractors in the area of the bait. This is a great tactic when casting single hook baits towards 'showing' carp. You can even wrap the paste around the hook so as to protect it as the lead and rig descend to the bottom.

WRAYSBURY
Another famous venue and one that will always have its place in carp fishing legend, not least because it was home to Mary, at one time the UK-record carp.

WYCHWOOD *(company)*
A subsidiary brand of Leeda, noted for its luggage, rods, reels, clothing and supplementary tackle.
Website: *www.wychwood-carp.co.uk*

XXX, ODYSSEY
Successful bait recipe from CCMoore. Odyssey XXX burst on to the scene and helped CCMoore – now a hugely established bait company – do likewise. It has accounted for numerous carp across the UK and the range includes everything from boilies and pellets to paste, dips, soaks and pop-ups.

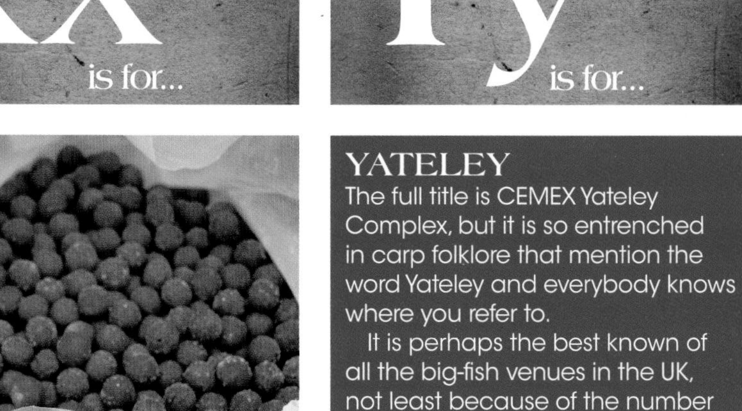

YATELEY
The full title is CEMEX Yateley Complex, but it is so entrenched in carp folklore that mention the word Yateley and everybody knows where you refer to.

It is perhaps the best known of all the big-fish venues in the UK, not least because of the number of big-name anglers who have devoted years of their lives chasing its residents and then writing many a book as they recount the tales.

Terry Hearn's book, In Pursuit Of The Largest is editor Marc Coulson's favourite carp fishing read and the stuff in there covering Terry's Yateley campaigns is beyond compare.

Situated in the small town of Yateley, on the Hampshire-Surrey border, the complex includes the hugely famous Car Park, North, Copse and Pads lakes, as well as the rejuvenated day-ticket water, South Lake.

Experiencing Yateley is one of those things, like golfers playing at St Andrews, that every carp angler should do at least once in their lives. Be sure to nip into Yateley Angling Centre for advice on how to fish each of the venues.

YEAST

More commonly, yeast extract is a popular bait ingredient and is found in many successful bait dips.

YELLOW

Although nobody has given the definitive answer as to exactly why, yellow is one of the most formidable bait colours known to the modern carp angler.

Despite its use on just about every lake in the country, and beyond, yellow just never seems to blow. Pineapple pop-ups (almost always yellow, of course) and sweetcorn remain some of the most effective baits there are, so perhaps there is something in the colour that carp find irresistible.

ZIG RIGS

Hugely popular method of carp fishing in the last five years or so. Essentially, zig rigging is fishing with a buoyant bait on a long hook link, many feet long in fact, to present a hook bait in mid-water. Essentially, the bait can be fished from a foot from the bottom right up to the actual surface using a zig rig.

The bait is anchored with a normal lead arrangement, such as a lead clip or helicopter rig, and can be adjusted to be presented in the same depth as the carp may be sitting in. On many lakes carp spend more of their time in various water layers than they do on the bottom or on the surface, so the zig rig has been developed to target these fish, which may otherwise avoid anglers' attentions.

As well as offering a food morsel in the form of a pop-up boilie or even a fly imitation or suchlike, some anglers believe that carp will take a zig-presented bait as much out of curiosity as anything else. Whatever the case, zig fishing is hugely effective and is very much here to stay.

ZIPP LEADS

These are a style of lead that were extremely popular in the 1990s, but which have been superseded by many more modern versions. However, leads of a similar shape to the originals – elongated and pointed at each end, ideally shaped for distance – are often still referred to as zipp leads, although they are made by an entirely different manufacturer.

NOW RUNNING ON
NEW GRANGE
mainline
RESULTS MACHINE
mainline
RESULTS